FOOTPRINTS IN THE SAND

A Lifetime of Poetical Musing-book one

Philip Carmen

Amazon

ISBN-13: 9798353059905
ISBN-10: 1477123456

Cover design by: Art Painter
Library of Congress Control Number: 2018675309
Printed in the United States of America

Dedicated to Dad- James Carmen, who tried as hard as he was able to make my childhood magical. Thanks Dad, for the memories.

CONTENTS

INTRODUCTION

I have lived over seventy years and over that
great span of time have experienced life in all its
splendour and all its pain and disappointments
yet can honestly say its has been a magnificent life
and my one desire is to experience more of it and
gain as much knowledge as my age allows.. This
first poetry and prose-at times autobiographical-
covers identity and childhood. I have had a varied
and interesting life spent in work and pursuits
that have added flavour to my life's menu. For a
large proportion of it I have been mentally and
physically disabled in one form or another, though
I do not want to harbour on about myself but try
to encourage others to take up the art of writing,
especially poetry as a form of therapy that will
stimulate and enhance their life in ways that they
cannot imagine. These last fifty years has been a
blessing in so many ways in no small part to my
wonderful wife and family who have supported
me in good times and bad. Having a degenerative
and very painful spinal condition has not made
life any easier at all and a mental condition of ASD
and OCD hasn't helped my situation, yet in life one
must endeavour to surmount the peak of ones'
afflictions and sour through the weight of gravity

that holds you down, finding the wings to fly. Being able to write and recently to paint has been my salvation; also getting out into nature. My wife Shirley is my reason to be and my life has been blessed beyond measure by her loving presence in my life. Within these pages is a lifetime of thoughts, observations and I hope will encourage people who find life just a little too hard to cope with. The second book which will follow shortly covers disability, trauma and fantasy. The third book endurance, nature and love. I hope you enjoy these little gems of escapism as I have enjoyed writing them, hopefully they will stimulate you to write your own poetry. Like me you may find them to be an avenue of light in a dark valley of suffering. Without creativity I would have sunk into the depths of gloom. With creativity my life has reached unexpected heights and experienced wonders.

Identity Crisis

Our identity is formed from the good times and the bad. Without the pain in life there can be little growth. Without the refining fire the perfect pot cannot be created. My life has been lived on the mountain top and the valley shadows. One cannot experience the heights of ecstasy without the darkness of despair. Life is made up of love and loss. I have experience both and would not have become the man I am without that experience. My parent had made a pivotal role in my development and I thank them from the bottom of my heart for their love. My dear wife is the source of my life and I would not have become who I became without her love. To be honest she saved my life. My children and grandchildren continue to inspire me to reach for heights that I would not have reached on my own.

IDENTITY

Sunlight shapes my identity.
Times all seeing gaze shapes my world;
dark shadows blur into insignificance
as I walk along a submerged Roman lane
back into a past filled with vague impressions,
on either side thorny bushes act as a windbreak
and I am channelled in one particular direction
as a lilting song that a minstrel sings,
cleverly telling a tale of days gone by-
Of errant lovers meeting in a secret rendezvous,
away from passing trades and curious eyes,
a beauteous maiden from the past,
a tanned young man of far future days
intersect in harmonious embrace
for a treasured moment in time.

PAST LIFE

Maybe I lived long before today?
Memories seldom ever go away.
Some are like reflections in a pool;
you try to touch but are not real after all.
I always wondered what the future must hold
as my past is often written bold.

Should I care after all when memories decide to
call?
If it is relevant, then let them be
simply part of my symmetry
or am I simply after all
reflections in another's pool?

Waves of time wash upon life's shore
yet I must know what I'm living for.
Is it such an indulgent whim my desire
to swim in memories stream?
Hopeful as I am to shed a little light
upon dreams I dream tonight.

Careful to not affect the flow
of memories I do not want to know
or idolize others, giving more power
than they should perhaps possess this hour.
Some memories I've discarded on the way;
others did not want to stay.

If once I could for a time impart

another's thoughts upon my heart
who lived so many lifetimes before
upon another's memory store,
wondering what he was living for.

GENETICS

Part of my identity is written into my genes by
my parents and grand parents. My grandfather
was born in Staffordshire in the 1870s. He
became a builder and worked for Mc Alpines
as a chargehand. At 38 he volunteered for the
First World War and joined the Royal Engineers
because of his working knowledge as a builder.
He survived the battle of the Somme as did my
mothers father who was also a builder, working
as a bricklayer in London, he was Jewish, though
not a practicing one. He built his own house in
Carshalton, Surrey where my mum was born.
My grandmother on my fathers side was from
Herefordshire and worked in service at the stately
home until she got married. My grandfather was
invalided out of the forces after being gassed on
the western front and started work after the war
as a hairdresser in Lind Road, Sutton. My father
joined the firm when leaving school and when
the Second World War began, volunteered in
the Dorset Regiment. My father served in North
Africa, Sicily, Italy and Greece until he was
hospitalised back to Banstead Mental Assylum
(during the war this establishment was taken
over by the military as a mental and convalescent
home) in England, suffering fro PTSD. This
affected him for the rest of his life. My mother was

a ballet dancer befor the war until she joined up to serve in the Womens Land Army. She married my dad in 1945. My sister was born in 1947 and I was born in 1951.

REGRETS

She came into my life
and I awoke,
a long, long sleep of absent longing.
She spoke,
like the clear waters of a mountain stream,
her lips not seeming to move
but her eyes saying what she wanted them to.
She gesticulated for me to come
and as if on a magic carpet
my feet moved hither towards her.
The nearer I got the further away she seemed
until I was left all alone,
and I slept.

CALM WATERS

Life's seldom
like calm
water,
whirlpools
and mistral
spray,
foam seahorses
waves
slowly
drown
your will,
send surfboard
thrills
flying
this
and
that
away.

ENDLESS SEA

For years my heart
has ebbed and flowed
like waves upon the sea.
They break upon
heartaches shore
and will not stop for me.

Will not stop the
seas cold rage
as memories of
another age
come flooding back
to me.

The tide comes in
and out again,
leaving me in my pain
and I am left with
a longing I cannot
quite name.

Now I wait, my love
for your return to me
across times endless, endless sea.

YOUNG AT HEART

If I had a rope
I'd find a tree.
It wouldn't matter
how wide or tall
as long as it were strong,
that's all that would matter
after all.

And swing as in
childhood days of yore,
swing from the self-same branches
that I'd swung from
so many years before,

and pretend
that I am Tarzan
or even Robin Hood
swinging free
from tree to tree.
For all that's good
in life is free,

and freedom
after all is when
you are young in heart
and all is exciting
from the start

and never ceases to be

as long as you have a rope
and can climb a tree.

MY SPECIAL HILLSIDE

How many years since last I walked
this woodland track, this hilly climb?
Is it really that many years?
Can it have been such a long, long time?

For I was nine years old then:
My friends, all three, were nine years too.
All of us possessed adventurous hearts.
We were a motley crew.

We crossed the road and over the stile,
ran down scampering lane and awesome view.
We hid in hazel and bluebell wood;
sought out pastures wild and new.

At farthest end of woody glade
the tower overhung the path like teacher's gaze.
We broke for cover before his eyes
onto grassy bank on our hillside.

We ran like the relentless wind.
We rolled on as the outgoing tide.
We had our youth and years ahead.
We flung all aches and cares aside.

Now as I look, I think I see the phantom shapes
of my friends and me an age ago.
I am no longer able to run, so I walk this hill
that bore my youth and watched it grow.

Little did we consider our future years
that stretched before us like the outgoing tide
locked as we were in childhood mode
and this was our own special hillside.

FRUSTRATION

Each way that I turn there is a cul-de-sac
with no opening anywhere.
Everywhere that I go I seem to bump my nose
on a door that is nearly always closed.

What is there that is so important to learn?
What good is this frustration in me?

I see anger arise like a beast from the sea.
I must vanquish it before it vanquishes me.

FAN THE FLAME

When I was young the fire was bright,
my zeal was fierce, my heart was light.
Now as I've grown my fire has grown dim,
burdens of life have quenched my flame.

A friend has come and fanned my flame,
thus, freeing me from all my pain.
He came to me, an encouraging glow
to rekindle hope, so help it grow.

For friendship is what we need.
Someone who helps is a friend indeed.
He gives me hope and helps me live
that I one day can help and give.

FRIENDS

The trees they bend
as friends to touch;
out of loneliness
they fear the time
when old and gnarled
they are not wanted,
beauty having faded,
branches sparser now
and not so heavy laden.

Yet how can I know
how they must feel
having come some way
along my street
and looking back
see many friends.

MEMORY OF YOU

Shall I depart now for some distant rendezvous? Memories of you will keep me from wandering aimlessly. Now I have somewhere to travel to I must arrive before its dark. Memory of you will keep me till eventually I embark.

For I have a one-way ticket that will take me to journeys end. You are in my thoughts always and will always be my friend. We have travelled long together but now I must journey alone.

Memory of you will keep me until I journey home.

MORE THAN CONQUEROR

You are all heart.
Your love soothes me,
caresses me and I am well again.

Love in the form of tears
combine to remove my fears.

Love in the form of words
command a blessing.

Love raids my fortress home,
tear out the bars from the windows,
unyielding, oaken door,
gaining entrance to my enslaved heart:

Making your home there.

UNITED

Am I simply a hollow shell washed
up along the beach of life?
No substance to my well
searching for some good advice.

Somewhere deep in the sea there
lurks the solid part of me,
separated from my shell and my life as well,
waiting for the tide to turn and
be re-united with my shell.

SURFING (CASCADE)

The sea churns away
inside as waves cascade.
Sand swirls around me
in my ancestral maze.

Seahorse waves tear
the fabric of me apart;
the cornerstone of which
is my hard beating heart.

Yet I will overcome
each and every tide,
surfing emotions waves

and shall never hide.

DREAMER

Come on dreamer, dream some dream
yet nothing comes to mind.
Sometimes it's like the blind leading the blind.
I wouldn't know if anything was in my way.
I would have to open my eyes to see what I need to
see
yet I'm still a dreamer of dreams,
so cannot discount anything by what they seem.

My song is sung to a different tune
and my journey is always only just beginning.
Before the words are heard my heart has already
begun singing.

For that is the way I was made,
to dream dreams bigger than me
and to bring them, by force, if need be,
into a real world of practical reality
not lost in a desert where nothing grows,
but springing from a constant spring of truth -

Given life and form by the words I say.

YOUTHS LAMENT

I used to wander as a child,
woods, hills and streams
my special hunting grounds.
No starched air for me.
I needed crystal clear air to feel free.
A solitary wanderer lost in childhood dreams
that never fully came to be.
Desperately desiring to fit in
I found myself alone once again.
Always alone with memories of my home,
wandering through a woodland view,
none to share and nothing new.
The summers hot once again.
It won't last long before another song is sung.
Winter has to come again,
dancing naked down some dishevelled lane.
I died when but a boy, yet here I live there still, as a
man,
with no life left, and no plan.
My life up to now a dream
with little reality in between
hills, trees and dancing stream.
Away in the meadow I lay my life down.
Can hear far away the haunting lament
of childhood spent in Sutton town.

CHRISTMAS TIME

Snowflakes settled upon my window like
diamonds reflecting off the streetlamp. Looking
across from my window I could see the first
workmen arriving to clock-in at the waterworks.
The men worked around the clock in shifts. Even
at Christmas ordinary people needed amenities
such as fresh water. The lamplight reflecting
off the water added a magical quality. The snow
settling upon the grassy borders created a fairy
paradise. The Newtown pub across the road
had been busy with rumbustious sights and
sounds, the breaking of glass in celebration
of something someone would forget after the
night of inebriation. Christmas lights flickered
on and off in tune with the neon sign. A cold
mackintoshes man with galoshes was sweeping
the pavement of the last vestiges of glass so
that some early morning dog walker would not
complain. Lind Road was empty of transport. Even
in the daytime few cars moved along the street. It
was a time of public transport and pedestrians, of
cycles and prams. I could just about see my school
from where I was sitting. Sutton East County
Primary School stood like a Victorian artefact
and if it could talk would speak of difficult times.
Times of learning, yet hard lessons learnt on the

battlefields of the brick walled playground. Of the strict code of teaching where you only spoke if you were spoken to, and of course the law of the cane and the slipper. I think that through this personal abuse we grew up with character, but at the time it was all about survival. Pretty girls that walked the streets were quite irreproachable. They were the gloriously clad damsels and one day I, a knight would appear out of the mist and carry her away upon my white charger. The smell of coal burning from countless hearths, through chimneys too numerous to mention. In the street though the snow was now settling there was a smoggy mist in the air. The radio was playing the first Christmas carols from the hospitals in the city, where the children in their sick beds were receiving their first and for some only presents.

A robin alighted on the windowsill, whose colour like a guard at Buckingham palace protecting the memory of what Christmas should always be. The assorted presents regaled in special paper lay in no particular order under the Christmas tree. The handmade multi-coloured chains bedeck the walls and across even the banister. The fairy on top of the tree looks down at me and I am in awe. The night before we had walked the lit-up streets, wandering with our eyes to spy on other neighbour Christmas fair, stopping only for a mulled wine and a mince pie at one of my father's friends. Small presents were passed out. Chocolate Fry's and Mars bars. Grownups spoke on future hopes while we children could only enjoy the present moment.

I had waited as long as I could possibly wait to open my pillowcase which being decorated with tinsel and hollow was holding my presents this Christmas time. The sound of laughter could be heard from adjoining bedrooms; and because of lack of insulation could be heard many houses down the street. The laughter was infectious and filled you with warmth that belied the freezing weather conditions. My heart will always be on fire, remembering the glittering times of one's childhood. The magic moments when parents held you close to them and spoke gladly of their deep affection. Treasures that cannot be bought yet lived again only though your own children's eyes in the many sparkling years to come.

ALSO-RAN

I ran into life and heard its tender voice
searching my heart and bidding me to come
running down the street of haggling men,
passed grizzled inns of hearty welcome
where at every turn man pulled my gown,
'Come this way', they called.

Not knowing where to go,
my face took on an irksome frown
for you see all of life held me enthralled;
I dare not, put my good life down.

Now tired and feeling like a sham,
I stop to reminisce.
Picking good parts from the span,
tossing away the bad like an apple core,
knowing without trouble life's a bore
and the rest an also-ran.

THEY CUT THE ROOT

They cut the tree down
on Saturday morn
A lifetime ago
I was born.
    A restless soul,
    an innocent child,
    bark began to thicken-
    I was wild.
Wild in the world
of make believe.
Roots went deep-
I did grieve.
    Grieve for a child
    lost at sea.
    Hair tangled wild-
    The child was me.
The tree deformed
grew out of whack.
The man alone wanted
his childhood back.
    They cut the living
part of me.

    Leaving my heart
    for all to see.
Weeds grew up
and vines took hold.
Before I was young
my mind was old.
    A shadow hangs over
    this wood of shame.

I am a number
with no name.
No name to call
my very own.
CUT AWAY FROM ME;
innocence gone.
A wood grew up
from a place called home.
I am forever
forced to roam.
There is little
bark left upon my tree.
Sadness and pain
must follow me.
Follow me down
a winding lane
leading the boy
out again.
Out from dreams
that did not come true.
Back from a past
he never knew.
They cut the root
down deep inside
leaving me
nowhere to hide.
The acorn fell far
from the tree.
No-one left
for me to be.
Myself a victim
of the fall.
All alone for
good and all.
The seed of life
fell to the earth.

PHILIP CARMEN

Giving the oak
its place of birth
among a forest
of its kin.
Waiting for life
to begin.

THE BOY LOST

The wood, it was my dark domain.
One day I entered as a child,
never to come out again.

No longer can I see the sun.
In this wood there is none.

As a child I lost my way among
where stoats and weasels play.

Tired and feeble I lay my weary head
upon twigs and leaves the oak tree shed.

The man at home under the hill
has only time left to kill.

The boy lost in the wood is gone for good.

The fox in his lair upon the hill
knows only fear and always will.

The man died alone under the hill.

The boy, lost, is roaming still.

THE VILLAGE GREEN

Now at a loss which way to go
a barrier has formed before my eyes
and past it is journey's end,
the latent heat, the village green and the sky.

Some recollections hold me up
so that I can look over yonder wall,
but see only emptiness and feel forsaken
as Prometheus in a deep dark pool.

While far away beyond the clouds
upon a village green, destitute and alone
lays a simple soul with just another hour to go
before him lays an open dream
and a loneliness we all do know.

CAGE'S

Strange,
to be walking,
always walking.
Lost in a zoo
with seemingly no way out,
only cages within.
Where even the seals look at you,
seeming to say, 'Are you real?'

But I am too close
to myself to understand,
therefore, stand and watch
the wind as it chases the waves
across the waters of my will
and ask the same question, 'Am I real?'
And are things really as they seem,
'Or am I trying to break out of a dream?'

Only to slip into questioning
what finding the way out of this
maze of thought may bring.

The cages crammed with animals
watching me without
from within.

EXPLAINING MY BODILY
SUFFERING AND MENTAL STATE

My mind is constantly thinking. It's like having
a constant conversation in my head without
an off-switch. At times it's like your head could
explode any minute. OCD is a crippling condition
but to me its part and parcel of being on the
autistic spectrum. Golly!! You obsess all the time.
Talk about being a hoarder. It seems like you
can never be satisfied with just owning a single
book volume in your collection. You need the
whole set. Your head goes berserk. You sweat
and are not satisfied until you complete the set.
Not necessarily to actually read the books but to
own them. After which you go on to your next
obsession. Compulsion is when you have your
foot on the pedal; but a normal person can stop.
This is a struggle (like a war) with someone with
compulsion as you have to fight not to put your
foot on the pedal and continue on and on. Do say
things other wouldn't say and do things other
wouldn't do. It is a constant fight. You are like two
people grappling with each other in a wrestling
match. When leaving my house, I am continually
(not so much now with medication) trying the
door to see if it is shut; even returning from miles
away to try the door once again. I have manic
periods which go sky high followed by really very

low periods of deep depression. Only in the last few years I realized that I ticked the boxes for a diagnosis of ASD. In some ways it is a relief. I can't change who I am but it certainly makes you feel different and being creative becomes a part of your make-up. So, I have accepted the state I am in; not looking upon it as a disability but a blessing. It is part of who I am- so I won't knock it. My PTSD/OCD medication helps to curb the worst of my symptoms: calming me down: slowing my brain down to manageable levels. My degenerative spinal disorder has limited my disability. I use to thrive on sport and fitness. Not able to exercise threatened my very sanity. My mind had to adjust and being able to write was not just a blessing but simply saved my life. Creativity is the wellspring that heals the body and mind and brings wellbeing to my soul.

CHANGING FORTUNE

Do you know the peace after the thunder?
Showers piercing thru your fragile gown;
fear rising against the flow of memories
that always let you down!

Wild nights where hard-fought victories are
known
and where wind rages without and within.
Terrors before unknown capture you in your sin;
mist curling like beckoning hands.

Surely someone must understand my life has
changed?

One moment there is sun then the rain.
One moment a kiss bringing release
and then the agony of parting!

When you left, I missed the touch
of your so soft hand against the parts
that brings tingling through my skin,
awaking a dragon deep within
that rises up within my heart.

By river bank where fireflies glow once we knew
what only lovers could possibly know.
A gentle spark that burnt apart
the wood of my imaginings,
and tears away my heart

by this deep, deep longing.

The peace I knew at the start
now torn apart like barns
along the Plain; bringing tornado pain,
heralding a change of heart,
maybe a fresh new start for the wanderer
who comes upon his love in the lane
and will never leave her side again

as long as there is sun and rain.

GOING BACK

They rounded a bend in the road.
A road that led down
long forgotten tracks.
Forgotten like a winters
seaside town.
I lived here once long years past:
Never should have come back.

The road led past a harrowed field,
lines of broken-down stone wall
and in the foreground a tattered town,
the patchy hill wearing it
like a tarnished crown

waiting for a pair of fools.

OUTSIDE THE WINDOW

Inside looking out, people walking: walking about.
Trees and grass so green, so very green,
the sun is shining and I am inside looking out.
They are outside living their own lives
without a thought to what I am about.

I enjoy just looking, for it is so easing to mind and
soul
but inside you cannot know or experience
life around you as it grieves and tries to grow.
Experience the sun against your face.
Experience the touch of growing things against
your skin
and the multi-layered sound of living.

To look with a creator's eye is not always enough,
one must also feel the gentle breathing
and many moods which whirl around you in a real
world,
flooding your senses with their desperate need.

COLLEY HILL

The winter wind is howling still
over the brow of Colley Hill.
Reigate town nestled down below;
two lovers keep a secret rendezvous
and I am young still.

Now I am older, where I have looked before
no curled smoke from steam engine stack passing
by.
Hurts of time has dimmed memories
of childhood rolling down grassy slopes;
the scent of grass opening to the flower.

Now as I look, I see the tower of refuge
in the midst of silver birch trees
and vast stretches of grassland over to the skies
edge
and beyond the Sussex Weald lies Brighton town
and seascape thirty miles away.

BEHIND THE WALL

I could not see her,
she being the other side of the wall,
but could hear her singing softly,
walking alone in the garden.
Heard her as her song rose and fell,
drifting into the treetops,
all was well.

Behind the wall
I dared not raise my voice
to sing a song in case
hearing me she might think me young
and clamber onto the top of the wall,
looking over to find an old man
praying for youth to come.

FORCES OF H2O

Leviathans of foaming waves
tower over my squealing head.
Waves grab at me and toss my solid flesh,
beach ward in one gasp of salt water and seaweed;
one gasp and then to sink
to the waiting sand beneath my feet,
while overhead another wave
travelling as a speeding train
breaks upon me as a flood,
rolling me as a pebble would
to dunes of sand and baking burning bodies
that sacrifice themselves to their sun god.

WAVES

The tides of our feelings
how they ebb and flow
from sea currents of gladness,
storm winds of woe.
Looking deep into her eyes
I see frothy waves of fear,
hiding doubt beneath
where no girl can steer.

Here on the surface
I feel he is scared
to admit his true feelings,
admit that he cares.
No one understands her
unless they look deep
within bleak sea caves,
her true feelings sleep.

We grab hold of the tiller
and steer to the shore,
for together we gain confidence;
can ride the storm's core.
Waves of our future;
undercurrents of our past.
Depths of our feelings
they surface at last.

CEMETERY

Leave me alone,
please let me be,
life is simpler
in a cemetery,
underground
with a stone above
a plaque,

"Here lies someone somebody loved."

Standing here
time stands still;
past and present mingle
and always will.

The dead surround the living;
those alive feel out of place;
this is nowhere to linger long:

Death has a many patterned faces.

ENCOURAGEMENT

Please encourage me,
I need a helping hand,
just a word will do.
Please try to understand

just as a tender plant
needs the rain
I need refreshing too.

MAKING PATTERNS

Making patterns in the sand
shapes seem to come unplanned.
Even more from movement of the wind
and the sea that seeps within

I made a shape of a heart
with the palm of my hand,
felt a restless beat
of life beneath my hand and feet,

knew I was one with
the earth and sun
the sand beneath my hand
are all somehow planned.

Deep within synchronicity
there is more to life
than you and me.

FRIDAY ST

I remember the place where once we met,
where our hearts still meet.
An older lady and a worshipful young man
walking hand in hand around the reedy pond,
at Friday St.
Halfway to Leith hills mountain tower
we met in an opening between close rooted trees,
there she held my hand and talked with me.

The fan-tailed ducks were feeding on
our bread we threw to them,
ducking and weaving to obtain the largest part.
In our own way we were ducking and weaving,
each in our own way not wanting to admit
or face up to what we both new to be true,
the end of our shifting and meeting in places
where people we both knew could never see.
We thought that in such a place our
fragile love could try to be.

The pond water broke as the ducks' found wings.
She looked into my eyes and I into hers,
both mouthing words we could not bear to be
heard-
Knowing this was to be our last meeting.

LEITH HILL

Friday Street

Lost in the midst of Leith Hill with beech trees and conifers surrounding lays supine and still an idyllic place of serenity and conscious peace; a place, which at varied times and at various phases of my life, I was drawn back to like a migrating bird returns to its breeding ground. Every time it was like the first time, for that is when I became locked in its surreal embrace. To me Friday St. marked indentations upon my soul, which as a tattoo will never fully fade.

In summer the willow weeps over the old green pond, populated by ducks, drakes, coots, moorhens, dragonflies and swans. Over in the furthest corner away from the public bar where the bank bends over, the reeds rustle and the lily flowers float upon the still water like a lover's bouquet. The needle points of streaming Tench bubbles surface like myriad air balloons. The water vole makes home beneath the thick rooted banks. The dragonfly hovers like helicopters in flight over the Lilly pads, settling for a moment, and then taking off again.

This was a place of many meetings, trysts and secret alliances. The wary looks from side to side, the older made-up lady and the younger man. The boy holds a fishing rod in his hands. The older sister pushes the pushchair in precarious places. The lonely and depressed their heads sagging into their chests. All types of people from every place are drawn like a moth to a light bulb. The pub that hangs its sign over the ancient bridge that faces the burnt-out lightning tree, and on the sign the picture of a tower and a pond and in old English lettering 'Friday St' of course. One can smell the tender scent of wild primrose flower; the bitter smell of hops that come by a pint measure glassful. Appreciative laughter mingles with the sad lament of a broken vessel.

Autumn comes and clothes this place in leaves. Winter comes and people leave; the pond ices over and the frosted Salix, its spindly branches hanging low into the water. Ducks skate in their hilarious fractured dance, finally to slop into a break in the ice's cold progress. A boy cracks the ice with a rock so letting the pond life breath. Heavy mitten and scarfed older lady walk's ever so intimately with the younger man, whispering quietly so no one else can hear or understand. There is the glimmer of firelight through the patterned windowpane of the public house; snow almost hiding the many trodden lane; skeletal tree forms bring stark relief; the horsewoman passing by admits a gentle wave; one hears the peel of bells from nearby Leith parish church calling its flock to thoughts of God.

Was I that young man, and was she that older lady
hand in hopeful hand?
Did we dare face the scorn of our fellow man only
to say adieu beneath the hanging Salix tree? Pond
life is the only life to see, also the tears that form
and fall into the cold and sleepy pool as the boy
and lady leave separately.

Memories of times gone by fool you as a man
remembering how life was as a boy. Broken
fragments as ice upon the pool tends to stay in
memories eye and attach greater significance than
I suppose was meant to be and never will be again.

THE HEART OF CHILDREN TO THEIR FATHERS

You judged me for what I was
not what I now am: I am a man!

The frail son that you knew before
was only like that for so short a time,
not more.

The person you held in your arms so long ago
no longer needs your help to grow.

But I need your friendship now
as much as I did when young;
now that I've grown into a man
who needs a father like a son?

GOODBYE DAD

Death is so final.
Death is so unknowable.
I cannot see behind the door,
the windows are closed,
the curtains are drawn.
He did not say goodbye,
he slept with life signs
making patterns on monitors
drugs pumped into distended veins:
blood being changed in calculating stages.

He was alive yet not alive.
He lived yet did not live.

We sat and waited,
speaking yet not knowing
we were being understood.
The sun went down and came up again.
Nurses being changed;
action's blurred in continual motion.

Dad passed the door.
He does not live here anymore.
I hold his ashes in my hands.

He longed to be a part of swirling rivers,
gentle streams.

This was all he felt he could understand.

to watch through Polaroid as fish darted
thru weedy tunnels, by rocky dreams.

When I was young, I was thankful to be
a part of his ideas and schemes.
We used to tramp the banks
and walk the overgrown pathways,
watching the sun timidly appear
in early morning when the world was new
and sounds were somehow clearer,
the air felt fresher and fresh hopes
peeped out from almost obscure places.

I was part of his world, probably I was his world.
A world where life could be lived again
upon a young child's shoulders; uncluttered brain.

His ashes run through my fingers; it looks
unchanged.
He is lost to us in this life,
his shadow will never cross our path again.

We remember him for his love.
Forget him in his pain.

I WILL WALK ABROAD AGAIN

We looked forward to this year
which will never come again.
Evening is drawing out.
Days are growing warmer.

The first rose to appear
left us floundering in regret.
One hopes before the year has ended
to see the leaves, turn yellow and red
before the Autumn Fall
gives way to Winter sparseness.

Yet, I will walk abroad again
into a new world my eyes
have not beheld before,
rejoicing with each step I take
before the Springtime thaw.

I will not take anything
for granted again
and will enjoy my health
as the young plant enjoys the rain.

HAPPY MEMORIES

Read a good book to me dad. You know which one; my favourite book of course, The Wonderful Wizard of Oz. You use to read it to me so often that I could repeat each sentence as you were reading it to me. I hear you laughing even now. "You do remember; don't you?"

You had so little time to spend with your family in those far off days yet you spent every spare moment that you could; working from eight o'clock in the morning to nearly seven at night in your barber's shop. I used to watch you as you concentrated on cutting customers hair. You did not always see that I was there. Indeed, you were a perfectionist even then. When we worked together decorating our house you taught me well so expected much from me but I so often came short of your expectations. Your love never once diminished though. It was not possible to have had a better dad, you know. Days on the riverbank together, fishing, are how I choose to remember you; seeing the look of contentment on your handsome face. The weariness of life washed away as you let the river work its magic on your soul. Nothing made you happier than spending time with me, and through the long years as I look back, I must admit to being never so happy since our all too brief times when the sun blazed a trail through the early morning mist; our faces sun kissed and feeling the weight of a fish on rod and line; your pride so obvious on your face when I won that fishing competition on The River Ouse at Tunbridge Wells. I was a mere boy of eleven at the time. You never seemed to care about yourself. All you cared about was that your son was with you and enjoying life. Letting your ashes fall through my fingers into the waiting water of river was a moment of pride and deep sadness; sadness at letting you go for a hopefully brief time yet pride in completing the task that you had given me as your last wish; to be in a place where you found the most peace. Dad, I hear your sigh even now and know you found release. Today I need to talk with you dad face to face, but you are not here in this place. The sun has set too quickly on our life together, yet I know in my heart that you, wherever you are, still care. I will always care for you and be proud to have been your son. Only memories remain but they are so real that I feel your hand upon my shoulder still. Know that a love so strong can never fade away, that one day we will embrace again as certainly as there is sun and rain.

COMPLETION

This picture, only paper now
yet any moment grows a flower,
a moment more as I draw a fairy glade
and could at any moment become so much more.
This picture holds the essence of my soul.
Colours mingle as the scene becomes more whole.
I persevere to paint the scene of where I might have been
once upon a time in a rhyme or wishful faded dream
that comes thankfully to completion in
a staggering moment of time.

IF ONLY

I left my youth behind when I grew old,
we parted where the crossroad ends.
I left my dreams unrealised and soiled
by Christianity and other things.

Where do I go from here?
Down the hill to some forgotten town
where the band still plays upon the square
and cricketers hit a ball around.

Back to my past there is a coal fire burning still.
I walk to school, satchel over my arm.
I see on my left-hand side the waterworks;
in the air I hear all too familiar sounds.

What would I have done differently
if only I had lived my life over again?
I would not tread the same old asphalt path
or hide my talents in my brain,

but would make sure my hands played a different
tune
and live my life for all its worth;
finding my path lit by neon signs:

The school where I grew up
is now a pile of trodden earth.

NO PRETENCE

I found a friend.
A friend who lightens
my darkest moments.
Alone, I sit
and am less afraid now
than when no-one was around
to dry my tears;
no-one to share
most thrilling moments,
deepest thoughts.

Everyone needs a friend,
otherwise, we would need
to pretend, invent a friend.
For that is what young children do.

My friend, I do not need
to pretend to you.

TEARS

The trees hang solemn like a mourner.
Grave still seems the wood in evening chill.
Paths meander aimlessly like spoilt children
and I am lost in shadows still.

There is no sound of laughter.
Nothing moves amidst this lonely undergrowth of
fear.
No friend holds out a helping hand:
No one cares for tears.

What it is to create

"How lonely are you, Robin?"
"Are you lonely, dear, as me?"
Maybe not exactly lonely, yet definitely
on my own, with very little chance of company.

I can think when on my own,
no-one to disturb my train of thought,
free to fly anywhere I think I ought or
simply to drift upon thermals, capturing my
creative bent, then ride it out till it's spent, until
the thought has flown its course, and paper looks
no longer blank and white, but etched with verses
that throb with a fresher
and more vibrant life.

CHILDREN EXPECTED

Children expected in a while,
in the turn of a smile
and at various stages
past a smile
to conception.

SHARED HEARTBREAK

There are so many times
where loves been bound,
crushed in unsympathetic surrounds.

Many times, and in so many ways
where the heart has felt the cruel jest
when loves betrayed.

So being cruelly dealt
the bitter straw of sorry wit
I can appreciate the fatal stroke
where love is torn and blooded
more than quite a bit.

FAITHFULNESS

A friend I knew was faithful.
In times of stress, he held my hand
and rejoiced and wept with me at will
and in many battles, we fought
together side by side.
Many victories, many disappointments, many
failures
but he took the other oar and we rowed in stroke.
My life I owe to such loyalty;
endows more to those who endure together,
honours best those who share the most.

MAKING WAVES

We make our own waves,
our own surf and spray.
The tide has turned at last
and you have turned my way.

For there is life beneath the foam,
silver flashes seen through transparent guise.
As I look at you, I see
watery tears fall from your eyes.

PLAYING FAMILIES

Peeling onions always made me cry
so did the stream of family visitors,
swapping comments on the fly,
"Can I take your hat, Uncle Sam?"
He held me like an octopus,
spreading his bulk as only he can;
crushing me like a tin of spam.

I looked starry eyed at Cousin Kate.
　　They all saw me as a child
　　but something stirred in the grate.
　　Mother gave me a knowing look
　　and continued to dress the turkey,
　　making sure the potatoes were chipped
　　whilst setting the oven to moderate heat.

At dinner I kept my eyes upon my overflowing
plate;
at times giving a coy glance at Cousin Kate.
She was breath taking to behold
and I wished that I were twenty years old.

　　The dinner came to an end.
　　Dad's belt buckle was undone, so
　　making room for him to bend.
　　Everyone felt lazy, the men retired
　　to slump in armchairs while the women
　　washed up while catching up on juicy gossip,
　　"Who was wearing what in their street of late?"

For this was half a lifetime ago:

Outside the window could be seen snow.
I took my sledge and slammed the door;
I could not have eaten anymore.
While sliding down the snowy hill
I thought of Cousin Kate and knew that I
would have to wait another year or two,
yet who knew what would happen then?

Snow blew into my eyes and I hit Old Tom the
tramp:
Falling arse over tit into a snowdrift and rued
the day I let my imagination run away.
    Life is a slippery slope and most of the time
    you need a rope yet I was so very young and
    all I could do was hope.

RAINY DAYS

Reach out and hold my hand.

We sit under a pergola,
sipping tea from a plastic cup.
Clematis and roses
climb artificial trellises.
There is a natural symmetry.
The colours collide,
purple, red, yellow and blue,

Darling, I cannot stop loving you.
We have unanswered questions
that will never go away.

The sun climbs higher into the sky.
Day is departing in shadows,
moving like feral cats

Does it have to end this way?

Lately we have come to expect
too much from one another.
Once, when we were young,
love was the song we sung.
Now you are content to let
our relationship drift along.
Content to let emotions hide
in some secluded garden shade.
Roses, perfect in beds new made.

I am not content to wait for the perfect day
that may never come again.
Clouds have passed before the sun.
What I always feared has come!

I crave the love that first we had
in garden days long and young.
When walking hand-in-hand
was something never planned,

but natural, like a bird-song.

THE SONG OF SELF

Save me from singing a song
I should not sing.
The bird in the treetop sings
a song made for it to sing.
It is beauty as the song
it sings is beautiful.

I will eventually become
the image of my song,
eventually will become as meaningful
as the song I sing, and as the bird
will wait for the dawning of a new day
with a joy that amounts to splendour
upon the tree of my surrender.

I await the morning,
when the morning comes
and will share with human kind
the song upon my tongue.

NO STRANGER TO A SONG

The ragged traveller with baggy knees
walks the avenue of trees.
His journey has been hard and long:
He is no stranger to a song.

He sings of encounters on the way.
Has many anecdotes to pass the time of day.
His journey has been hard and long:
He is no stranger to a song.

Now his journey is coming to an end.
Old age is approaching, he is frightened.
His journey has been hard and long:
He is no stranger to a song.

Now he has laid his troubles down.
Peace at last he now has found.
His journey has been hard and long:
He is no stranger to a song.

There is no travelling anymore.
He rests at last on the father shore.
His journey has been hard and long:
He is no stranger to a song.

RETURNING AND REST

The virgin snow falls crisp and white,
so, my love I leave tonight
on unbroken highways,
sheltered by ways,
in secret and in quiet.

By morning I will find my way;
there is solace in a fresh new day;
and we will meet again
down some deserted lane,
all hurt cleansed from my memory.

MISSHAPEN (SHAPES)

"What shape is that, daddy dear?"
To me it's not so clear.
It is round, but so are roundabouts.
Coins are round,
but so are my tear-filled eyes.

The world has such interesting shapes.
My room is a rectangle
and from this particular angle
so is the picture I keep of you.

When you left, I thought my heart
would break in two.

Our house is shaped like a box,
where mummy, Debbie and myself fit.
"Why has the shape of my world changed?"
I do not understand that a bit.

Daddy, you shaped my world,
and all that my eyes surveyed,
please, come back, put us all together,
I feel so misshapen and so afraid.

My world, all that I comprehend,
is shaped for you and mummy,
Debbie dear and me,
I need to feel us back together again,

living in family harmony.

What shapes your life doesn't
necessarily shape mine
but without you
a piece is missing:

The Sun cannot possibly shine.

AN OBSERVATION

The door opened,
three families walked in,
each sat at tables on each
corner of the dining room.
Each family settled into their cocoon.

The door closes
and the room fills up with whispers.
So hemmed in you become, as the four walls closes
in,
that one is reminded of existing in a tomb
with not even a "pass the salt, please"
or "thankyou" to be heard
over an Englishman's unnatural reserve
with each couple trying as hard as they can
not to clink the plate with a spoon;
to do so would sound like thunder
in this gallery of faces where few words are spoken
but much is presumed.

THE CRICKET FIELD

On my own in the middle of a cricket field,
nobody around to call out my name,
no one to clap when I score one hundred runs,
and when I'm caught out, no one to blame.

When your bats on the crease the ground
stretches out as far as you can
see away to the boundary,
to suddenly wonder why
there are no spectators here to see
the endless game going on endlessly.

Nothing moves out in the ground's extremities,
not even a bat hitting a ball.
Not even the referee shouting "it's four":
For there is no referee anymore.

There is only an old man living out his time
in a dirty old bedsit, drinking bottles of wine;
dreaming of a past that was only ever in his mind.

SLOPES

I have chosen the slopes to rest my head.
Deep down the valley was my bed
and I was tired and poorly led.

Upon the slopes, the hill that shades my sanctuary
man was made to climb and reach for victory.

Seldom now do my eyes stray down
to look into the valley town and see the lights
and wish to be locked up in my privacy.

LOVE CONQUERS ALL

No shadows linger in my mind.
The sunlight today has been so kind.
For a time, storm clouds held the sun at bay
now your love has wiped my tears and fears away.

My heart no longer burdened by remorse.
Your love will guide me in life's course.
Rays of sunlight disperse all my mortal fear.

I know only love when you are near.

RICH

Who are you?
Are you me?
Sitting there
so fancy-free.

Are you rich?
Are you a king?
Is it true that you can sing?

I can sing.
Yet I'm not a king,
Still, I am rich;
I've always been.

Rich as any
man could be
who has the gift of life
and eyes to see.

WINDOW-SHOPPING

The lady is lonely,
lonely as me,
we sit at opposite ends
of the same tea room
looking out of the window
hopefully,
yet still we do not see.

SIMPLY NOT A DREAM

She sings on bank where willow sweep
her fronds along the verdant stream.
Her music is sweet to the ear,
sad and plaintiff, yet sincere;
seeking only to redeem, only to redeem.

For hard times had broken her tender heart
and she fears the hurt will not depart.
She speaks as one who has felt
the storm as well as the sun.

She says "Can this be all that I can glean
from life's rich tapestry?

"Surely there is someone somewhere for me,
who will have their own song to sing,
and can take this burden held so long,
and cast it off into the stream?"

The sun rises over the water cool.
The first leaves have begun to fall.
The meadow lark sings of days long gone.
Nature knows there is magic in a song.

Nature knows and I do too
that rising up within the heart of you
is love enough in winter's chill to
melt the ice from off the stream,
make even the broke-hearted beam.

I've seen you have within your power
the heart to make all men flower.
If they could only look then they would see
a radiance shining forth from thee.

She sings on banks where willow sweep
her fronds along the verdant stream.
She knows somewhere that he is waiting
to make her life complete,

and he is simply not a dream.

COMMITMENT

As I walk with you, love
my needs are met,
the road less rugged;
no need to fret.

As I talk with you
all self-thoughts flee,
my eyes fresh set
on only thee.

ALL MANNER OF THINGS

There is so much left
for us to see,
the sky above,
below,
the sea
and in between
all manner of things
try to be.

TIME

I wish I could recapture time,
yet once it's gone, it's gone.
The summers past, the winters come.
The rain is here, the sun once shone.
Yet my memories are mine, and only mine.
The sun once shone and once again will shine
upon a new dawn, a new day that is sure to come
my way.

For now, I hibernate in bliss remembering last
night's kiss. Remembering all the good that's gone
before;
the swans upon the river Itchen giving birth;
white waves at Bournemouth rolling onto shore.
New places that I've been, seen and shared with
the one I love are planted forever in my brain to
recollect for all time like moving pictures on a
movie screen;
so, forgetting all my present tears and pain.
This year to come will bring to us a richer store of
memories that are sure to surprise and to enthral
as no other year before.
New buds upon the apple tree, colourful blooms
for us to see; fresh possibilities to share and
renewed
commitment; loves answer to prayer
As we embark upon this virgin shore that none of

us has seen before I do not know at what cost and
in what shape or form it will come to be.
Only know that it will be the future we make it;
one day our history

BRUSH STROKE

'You really must not lay this canvas down!' the
pallet cries. Brushes stroke away all marks of self-
pity.
Of course, there is sadness!
Then again there is tenderness.

Darkness and incorruptible light fight
for your considerable attention;
battling for a point of entry.

'Can you see him?'

'This solitary figure walking in a landscape of your
own making; lost in a world of make-believe.'

TREASURE

She looked so sad, so very sad,
like a slightly disarrayed Cindy doll.
Her head was held in her hands,
slightly askew as if she was trying
to place it back on her body.
One solitary tear hung down
the precipice of her
perfectly positioned cheekbone.

If only I had been there to catch her
as she swung too far out into the unforgiving
air
and fallen in slow motion like a feather
yet hitting the ground like a stone.
Her cries were resonant and heart breaking.
My arms that held her trembled;
she, like a fragile precious treasure.
Her future spanning the years before her,
full of promise, so full of promise.

I realized more than ever I needed her
with all her pains, whims and ways
and on her part, she needed me,
especially at this moment in time
to take her in my arms and wipe
her tears and fears away.

TRANSPORTED

You transport me to a high mountain
sending me on a journey into a deep sea.
You cause me to look afresh at expressions;
ideas that mill around my mind
are circling in the coral reef of inspiration.
Multi coloured facets shine like diamonds
and reveal a fresh face for me to see,
a face that I have never seen before.

Is there is no end to this menagerie of sensations?
One has but to hold a pen over a piece of paper
and write down what magically records itself-

What can be more wonderful than that?

THE HEART TO TRY

Sometimes I fly
but that happens
less frequently now
than it used to.
   There was a time
   when I thought
   I would fly forever.
   The air about me
was clear, uncluttered;
no storm clouds on
my horizon threatened
to appear.
   But now my mood
   has changed.
   There are clouds as far
   as my eyes can see.
   What the future holds
   has become a mystery.
I remember once
Imagining I could fly,
but now
I no longer
have the heart
to try.

SLOPES

I have chosen the slopes to rest my head.
Deep down the valley was my bed
and I was tired and poorly led.

Upon the slope; the hill that shades my sanctuary
Man was made to climb and reach for victory.

Seldom now do my eyes stray down
to look into that valley town and see the lights
and wish to be locked up in my privacy.

SMALL FIRES

I hope I am fruitful.
That I do not just exist
in existence.
I am satisfied
as long as I am
producing.
It does not have to
be much to be
an inspiration.

We need small fires
lit by others
to encourage us
to light fires of our own.

THE STREAM

The little stream hides from curious faces
amongst the woodland greenery,
slivering like a grass snake,
shining only where the sun
finds it glistening in an open glade
where a man and women
upon lush bank lay supine,
almost a part of its symmetry.
They writhe in motion with the wind,
their hands exploring secret indentations,
sweaty bodies matted by grass and the warm earth
of their own special trysting place.
Not giving a single thought at that moment
to where life's stream goes;
not caring if they are seen or heard.

A LITTLE WHILE

Dark and foreboding is this place bereft of heat,
soul and grace wearing a grimy, dusty coat.
Cobwebs littered, bespoke of times when mind
enchant,
I fear to look, my mind can't focus in this wretched
place,
of feelings of disgrace.

I hear whispering in the dark yet my spirit must
embark
on a journey from here to there upon a traveller's
prayer.
Hopefully calm waters will I find upon the journey
of my mind yet I tremble, once looking back, to see
my fear attack the feeble form my life took when
trying to write a little book.

When I was green and in my craft, I laughed at
shadows cast in the corner of my mind where, as a
poet I would find solace from a line of thought that
I hope one day is bought from a bookstore in the
mall.

Yet is it mine to sell at all, these random thoughts
that run around my brain and will never come
again?

There must be solace in a rhyme.
I fear I have no longer time to make a parchment of

my mind, keeping all the thoughts I find on every continent, across every sea where my heart hopes to be.

The only way now that I can go is in imaginations flow
for I am tied with ropes of fire, having the heart but not desire.

So much more there is to know if I am allowed to travel this life's flow.

Yet time for me is fading fast, so I must make my fortune last another day, a week or two, until I bring it home to you.

There you wait and in a little while I will meet you with a smile.

YOU

Am I really real?
What does reality mean
to someone like myself
drifting between love and a dream?

Reality to someone like me is more
than being able to see, touch or smell
yet what is reality to someone like you,
who knows me so well?

The one thing I know is that I love you so.
To touch you sets my heart aglow
and the scent of you is more fragrant by far
than all the flowers in the world.

And when you are not with me,
to know you is enough-

That will have to suffice for now.

LOST

Years ago, I lost my way
on moorland paths
one autumn day.

One winter's day
a year ago
I found a path
through drifts of snow.

The path led down
tomorrow lane
ending my life of pain.

THE MARKET

I can hear Pipes of Pan playing in the market square
where haggling is the only way to sell one's wares.
The unpitying sun bakes you to the pumice stone;
Amidst legions of people, you can feel all alone.
I hold you by the hand, for you see, my whole world consists of you.
Shirley, you are the only person that I truly understand.
My love like boiling lava flows, my temper erupts like a volcano.

This is Lanzarote, where locals speak Spanish and where English is frowned upon.
You lose your grip of reality between a theatrical arm wave and simmering stares.

Lavishly dressed African women braid young girl's hair.
They do this all day long from sun-up to sunset.
Suited Spanish men pester you to buy video cameras
which magically lose value before your eyes.
Handbags open, money changes hands.
Currency is euros, though the seller is flexible, por favor;
pleasantries are spoken followed by gracias,

mochas gracias.

On the corner a gypsy woman reads palms to
gullible tourists, as two clowns tumble in the
square.
Yet it is the hurdy-gurdy music of the carousel
that enchants my mind.Instantly I am a child
again, holding onto daddy's hand.

I sit in the sun burning like a mad Englishman.
Opposite us is the Roman Catholic Church with its
dedicated priest preaching to his flock.
He is dressed in clerical raiment's and wears a
respectful frown whilst multinational, bilingual
tourists drift past like spectres.

I think I see sadness in his eyes.
Is he remembering older days when the streets
were uncluttered of tourists, but full of sheep.
When young people were respectful
and the old looked up to you.

He loves to recall that his grandfather lived
through
the eruption that covered the Island in ash:
larva hardening to pumice.
Now the buildings are built of the same material
and the same ash floats in the windy air.

At nights the cockroaches hide from inquisitive
eyes,
and skinny cats slink through the ash black fields

hunting for food, the fishermen tell wonderful tall tales deep into the night as the fires burn in the hearth and the old man plays flamenco on his old guitar.

THE BOWLING GREEN

The green lays quiet
before the tide of bowlers
bowl their finest bowl.
Fresh cut the emerald green
before the rush of busy feet;
from novice to veteran,
bouncer to an easy roll.

'The green is running fast'
a bowler says, and with a
disarming roll surrounds the jack.

With a final bowl, leaving
little room for others to improve upon.

At night, when all have left
this sanctuary of divine conquest,
the green takes on a solemn sheen.

At mornings light dewdrops lie across the green.

WHAT MIGHT HAVE BEEN!

Grave still the room at dead of night
where you unwrapped your present in my sight,
shook loose your garments and let them fall;
so emotional yet intangibly cool.
You gave a backward glance as if to say

"Come: for it is your birthday".

With this gesture of a kind
she stormed the temple of my mind.
It should have been so easy then
to handle the part where true love stems.

Out of the corner of my eye
I began to question why
this worldly system that seemed real to me
was simply a remnant from my memory.

For I was remembering loves first fling,
now that I'm old, my body wasting.

Feelings that stir when the mind has dimmed
the candle of what might have been.

WINDOW-SHOPPING

The lady is lonely,
lonely as me,
We sit at opposite ends
of the same tea room
looking out of the window
hopefully, yet still we do not see.

SUNLIGHT SERENADE

The sky is paved with darting light the
like of which I may never see again,
for in this dustbowl of my heart
I need the flow of tears to start
before I wake to know my worth
amid this canyon of my birth
where I see a mirage of a lake of light
lying restless before dark banks of night,
amid this canyon where I was born
among the desert cactus thorn
which pierce my growing wrinkled skin,
leaving their poison deep within.

Yet, in the blushing sky I come to know my fate.
For life has been tough on me of late.
Why can I find no harbour for my soul?
Maybe all my hurt has worked to make me whole
having purged the worthlessness out of me;
leaving me thankful for who I have come to be,
thankful for the sights and smells;
the rawness of the deserts fiery air,
the translucent, restless sky-

Satisfied with who I truly am
and even the clothes I wear.

REMEMBER SUTTON

Remember Sutton.
Reach down memory lane
to childhood's mystery path
that runs through the dark wood
of my yesterdays.

The dark wood of my soul;
the shadowy hollows
between mossy banks
where I rested my head
in far distant days,
and always looked forward;
never fully satisfied
to simply be me,
enjoying each and every moment.

The boughs of the trees
bowed down and stealthily grew
tangled in my consciousness.
My dark world within
hemming me in.

And so, I was lost,
and thereafter could find
no pathway that led
to the rest of mankind.

SUNLIGHT ON THE BAY

Light upon the water.
Light upon the sea.
Hope, the candle lit each day.

When I remember
I will light a candle to you.
Dreams unfold through life
and some of them come true.
As you grow old and your candle grows dim
I will light another candle in passing.

Remembering times gone before.
A pair of footprints on the shore
that led along the bay wherein rock pools
of still sea water lay.
You picked up a shell and put it against your ear,
hearing the sound of the sea over your fear.
Foaming seahorse spray chase
dreams and memories away.

The smell of seaweed capturing for a time,
power of recall hidden in the salty brine.
Now the sea washes our footprints away.
A lot of time has passed today.
Even more in memories store
when life had so few certainties;
yet none appear anymore.

Never again will I know
the wonders that the sea bestows
upon seeing eyes and listening ear.
For me there may not be another year
as the past fast catches, up on me.

Fortune once smiled on the things
we used to do-

All I really want in life is you.

WASHING BASKET

Shirt arms
hangs limp
from under
the lid.
    The hallway
    light shed
    colours
    that moved
    across
    the arm.
My sleepy eyes
as I crossed
the hall to
the lavatory
fooled
me.
    For you see
    I thought
    I saw the
    arm move,
    ever so
    slowly
    at first.
The lid to
the basket
suddenly
burst open
and the
shirt rose,
billowing
as it moved,

threateningly,
towards me.
    Forgetting a
    pressing need
    for a pee
    I raced back
    into my bedroom,
    pulling the
    covers over my head,
    waited for the arm
to reach inside
and...........
    But I was only nine
    at the time.
    Last night
    I was sure
    it happened
    again-
I was nine once more;
at least in my head.
This time I did
not feel safe
in my bed.

COCOON

I form in this cocoon
between one moment of thought and the next,
straining against a meshwork of impressions,
finally breaking through a latticework of ideas,
flying forth on gossamer wings,
so easily disarming your criticism with majestic
beauty;
bringing forth realization in your eyes.

FORCES OF H2O

Leviathans of foaming waves
tower over my squealing head.
Waves grab at me and toss my solid flesh
beach ward in one gasp of salt water and seaweed;
one gasp, and then to sink to the waiting sand
beneath my feet, while overhead another wave
travelling as a speeding train breaks upon me as a
flood,
rolling me as a pebble would to dunes of sand and
baking burning bodies that sacrifice
themselves to their sun god.

RAINDROPS

Raindrops
fall,
pit-a-pat,
pit-a-pat:
Refreshing
me.
　Under
　protective
　tree
　canopy,
　I lie,
watching
scurrying
waves
on the
river
flow
by.
　My
　mind
　escapes
　as a bird
　into the blue
　and tainted sky.

FORGOTTEN

Years ago, I lost my way
on a moorland path
one Autumn Day.

One winter day
a year ago
I found a path
through drifts of snow.

The path led
down a forgotten track.
I will not be coming back.

A FRIEND PASSING BY

She left today-
Another friend who passes
by in life like a song
you once knew so very well
but now the tune seems wrong.

CHANGES

I always said the world will change
before I'm very much older
but if I change before
the world changes
so much the better!

ON THE SLIP ROAD

Spent most of my life off the highway;
on the slip road between the hard shoulder,
and the bye-way,
off-times finding the comfort of lover's lane
or the track that leads off the cinder track of pain.
So set in my ways with little sense of progress.
Surely there must be a track that hurts you less?

On the hard shoulder I see signs of lives broken
down.
Families wrecked by insensitivity and lack of
respect,
people constantly wearing a soulful frown,
no-one seems to smile anymore, they say,

'What is life really for, if it lets you down?

Some have taken the wrong junction,
ending up on the verge of a nervous breakdown.
They wait forever for the tow-truck:
Yet of their own lives they have no plan

Yesterday I managed to get off the slip road.
For me the highway runs straight and true.
Still, I am in danger enjoying it so much
that I miss the view.
Life passes on either side. You see:
On the highway there is nowhere to hide.

Those fanciful days are long gone-

I might as well enjoy the ride for as long----

RETURNING

I had to return sometime, now seemed as good a time as any; but was I prepared in my own mind? Would it be the same as I remembered it? How long ago was that? The time escapes me as does the years. Fragments of memory locked away in the mind's archives.

Last time I was nine. Three friends and a boxer dog called Butch accompanied me on another adventure. For every new place we visited was an adventure in those far off days. The stile looks to be the same, though weathered and worn like myself. The bluebell woods are no longer there. The hazel trees full of nuts, the woody smells and the bluebell carpet. It was all so fresh and at the same time mysterious. My senses are showing the first signs of deep loss for my fondly remembered bluebell wood has been replaced by an ugly gash of a motorway flashing across my line of sight into my conscious mind.

A bridge spans an ugly road, a means to get to Colley Hill, yet before I see the hill I see the water tower, broken and old when first I had set my eyes upon it; now so much older and broken beyond repair. Yet the sight of it awakens my sensibility.

At one time, long ago it was a doorway to another

age and we would run; three friends and a dog in tow. Now I walk; my two girls break free and run, as I had run in more youthful days to see over the brow of the hill.

What sights they will behold? The grassy outreaches, the flowing stream, the meandering road, the vast expanse of hills in the distance before the inevitable seaside view of ancient Brighton town. Mists still curl around housetops in Reigate vale. I remember the smoke billowing from toy steam train-for that is the way it looked to me when I was young. Obviously, time has changed the picture some, and all I see now are buildings, steeples and automobiles- so many automobiles. They correlate in mind's eye yet do not ring true to my memories.

Perhaps my children will experience their own sensations. I must remember to talk to them about it when we get home. I am not disappointed, for I have been on a journey of rediscovery. My life is full of new and exciting experiences- the old making up my understanding of the world I now live in.

CHILDHOOD IDYLL

Katy and Debbie like to make patterns in the sand; patterns that grown-ups cannot possibly understand.

'In a wonderland they lie,
Dreaming as the days go by,
Dreaming as the summers die;
Ever drifting down the stream-
Lingering in the golden gleam-
  Life, what is it but a dream?'

Lewis Carroll from Alice through the Looking Glass

THE CHILD IN ME

The child in me cries out,

"Where is the land I dreamt about?"
A fairy land where the Pied Piper plays his tune:
Where grown-ups do not belong.

In my skin I am a man, inside not grown.
This world has become too complicated for me.
There is a world only I can see,
a magical world only I and children know-

The other end of the rainbow.

THE EYES OF A CHILD

Through the eyes of a child
waves crash upon the beach
like white maned mares with riders.

Fortresses of sand dare
the invaders to breach the walls.
The work of many hours of labour
dies defiantly but not finally
until an Alexander comes and history recalls-

Build up the walls as they were at last
using only a bucket and spade
and an imagination lacking in grown-ups.
For they see only sand and sea
not adventure and mystery-

Seeing not what children see.

CHILDHOOD GONE

How disappointing now to find
no magic land beyond the trees.
No tower from which Rapunzel
let's down her hair.
No, nothing but despair and more despair.
  Oh, so disappointing to find
  no Wonderland down a rabbit hole.
  No Mad Hatters tea party.
  No dormouse in the sugar bowl.
  Never will I feel so whole again.
  Only left, despair and pain.
No Father Christmas with his sleigh.
No World of Oz at Rainbows End.
No elves and fairies to call my friends.
Even my teddy bear has lost that soulful stair.
Is there nothing that makes amends?
  Childhood gone like a puff of smoke!
  So, wish I possessed the Genie in the lamp;
  rubbing it would make this fantasy never end:
  This land called 'let's pretend'
  where Bambi was my friend.
But grown-ups lose their magic cloak
and end up telling silly jokes, so
losing their innocence in the end.

A GIRLS BEST FRIEND

Everywhere I go you must go too,
even into this water so blue.
You go first and I will follow in a while,
squealing with the cold yet wearing a smile.

First, we must put on these rubber floats
So, we can move like little boats
over the sea and far away,
where friends like you and I do play.

Everywhere I go you must go too
even into this water so blue.
You will always be my best friend;
with you it's so easy to pretend.

Life is so pleasant in your company;
God must have made you just for me.
Sitting here, holding your paw
life is so worth living for.

Everywhere I go you must go too,
even into this water so blue.
I am afraid to go in on my own-

We will swim together till I'm grown.

SNOWY TOPIC

To break the cycle
I find myself walking
In the woodland of my mind:
I am a child again,
dragging my boots
along snowy tracks
that leaves their mark
for so short a time
before fresh flurries
rub them out again
like an eraser on paper.

Trees look down scarily.
Their branches like brown fingers
trying to gain a hold
on my tender psyche

I hear the scurrying feet
of fearful invaders hiding out of sight
yet still infecting me with alarm.
I try so hard to face down the intruder
in my much too tender mind.

As an adult I see the boy falter
on the path to maturity
but am unable to help him
as he is a soul alone, lost,
unable to find the path

that leads out of this tangle of confinement;
this heinous vegetation that harbours
harm toward all of human life.

So, the boy must continue to march
forth upon a chilly journey
that may or may not end successfully.

The boy catches a glimpse of the adult
through the barren wastes
that is his unconscious mind,
see that he must continue
through the hinterland of his fears,
to eventually break the vicious cycle
keeping him prisoner there.

BOY

The blistered sea magnificent
beneath many patterned skies.
Rays of gladness filled my soul
not known since a boy.

The boy stayed the same
within cold archives of my brain,
leading my thoughts and schemes
into a labyrinthine maze of incessant pain.

Ah, innocence of a youthful mind
where responsibilities made nil and void.
He leads me through rustic wood
So, bypassing the urban crowd.

I came here from far distant land,
beside a tumultuous Bering Sea,
my heart beating in your hopeful hand
knows who I am, and what one day will be.

MEMORIES

I walk again down half remembered tracks
through oak wood silence and bluebell carpeted
where squirrels leap playfully in the treetops.
I cannot hear my footfall against rooted earth,
see mossy imprints, smell familiar impressions.
For this is memory stored within my brain;
archives for my lifetime only.

I remember, two friends for company.
A dog by our side, a smile on spotty faces:
and the Joy of a shared adventure.
We reach the water tower together, then
onwards to the lip of the grassy sloped hill.

Looking down from where I stood,
see spiralling smoke from a steam train.
For this was a different time;
a more relaxed pace of life.

I was locked in childhood's mode.
I was following that particular pathway.
I switched paths when I was thirteen.
I am not allowed to walk that path again-

Not in my lifetime anyway.

HOME

Once it stood in splendour but now it is a ruin.
Each room knew love and laughter. Now only
copious amounts of dust and cobwebs are strewn
willy-nilly. Yet I remember once being a child here,
being lifted in my father's arms. Home was where
I knew that I was cared for, protected from hurt
and harm. The walls, if they could speak would tell
their tale too.

I walk past the broken gate and through the
unhinged door. The smell of decay assaults
my nostrils. I could cry such is the scenes of
desolation that I see before me but my childhood
home reaches out in greeting as if it recognises a
kindred spirit as I wander through each memory
clad room and up disjointed stairs to my bedroom
that now wears pauper clothes and marks if
disarray. No glass is left in the wood windows and
I almost turn my head away but for the sound
of a bird singing from the ancient oak tree bring
memories flooding back to me of how things use
to be back down the back alley of time.

Once this building that I once called my home
was vibrant with life, laughter, crying, sadness,
arguments and making up-all that pertain to
family life; the nostalgic smell of roasts permeate
through the house; the aroma of chestnuts
roasting on our coal fire at Christmas; the smell
of Dad's favourite smoking tobacco issuing like
smoke signals from his favourite pipe; the scent of
Mum's favourite perfume that Dad use to buy her

on her birthday; fresh cut flowers harvested from our garden left their own rich heritage. Our pets made their own indelible marks upon our lives. Such sensations envelope me like a warm dressing gown. I close my eyes, remembering the happiness that I once knew in a happy home. Home, such a beautiful word; home is where true love is shed; home is this searcher seeking solace and lasting peace; home is commitment and soul release.

KATY SAID

Katy said,
'Daddy, if you lift me
high enough, can I fly?'

Looking back to my childhood
had my Daddy lifted me high enough
I believe I could have flown

but it's too late now I've grown.

LULLABY

She pulled back the curtain
to let the day in,
The sun said, "Good morning, Katherine."

The wind called
"Good morning to all who can hear,
especially to you Katherine, my dear."

WAR IS HELL!

I used to play at war
when I was young,
now I know war is hell:
It is not fun!

I picked a stone and stick
on Epsom Downs
and it turned into a rifle round.

In bygone days
we played to win.
Today we say,
"This war is not sin!"

I hid in the bushes while
My friends tried to find me.
Today, in Ukraine
they call them the enemy.

I must admit,
when I was young
playing at war
was not much fun.

A stone from a catapult
can sting your leg
but today in the Ukraine
you end up dead

After playing war was done

when I was young,
we ate bars of chocolate while
passing Tizer around, not a gun.

"This war is just."
the invaders say,
yet the innocent does not
want to play.

I used to play war
when I was young,
now know the truth:

No wars are really won.

A LILLEY IN A STREAM

Let me take you by the hand
sweet Katherine.
Let me try to understand
sweet Katherine
why you affect me as you do,
or why my heart is full of you.

Your soft blue eyes like silent pools,
your laughter is like a waterfall.
I am impatient to see you grow
sweet Katherine,
but also desire to stop the river flow,
just for a little while,
to linger longer on your smile
sweet Katherine.

Yet you cannot understand as yet
how much to you I mean,
you, like a perfect Lilly flower
floating in a stream.

NOT HOT AIR

Debbie made a hot air balloon today
out of a supermarket food box and lots of string,
white sticky tape and things, a big hot air balloon,
blanket and sheet, teddy bear and Cindy too;
and to the entire world she swore
that out of the door and into the air it flew.

With all my faith in her I swear I saw it too.

THE CHILD AND CRICKET

On my own in the middle
of a cricket field.
Nobody around to call out my name;
no-one to clap when I score one hundred runs;
no-one to hear if I call out your name.

When you're on the crease
the field stretches as far as you can see
away to the boundary.
Nothing moves, only silence
that pervades to the extremities.

Even a whisper would seem
like a bat hitting a ball.
"Four", shouts the fielder out at mid-on.
Slowly the clapping and silence mingle.

I am six again with my life still to run.

THE MONGREL AND THE BOY

His friend is hairy with a tail.
Tom holds him very tight.
He knows Bobs love will not fail
but will keep him warm tonight.

Tom has been let down before.
So many times, trust has been betrayed.
Bob knows- Holds out his paw -
Tom's troubles to rest are laid.

Tom had a home but ran away
after suffering constant abuse and pain.
Bob, the ill-treated stray
was given no choice but to run away once again.

They met in the park where children play:
Two lost and lonely strays.
Together, they hope for a search light
that will lead them through life's cold maze.

The canopy of leaves shields their eyes
from the suns relentless stare.
Innocence will have to be a disguise
for this odd companionable pair.

IMAGINARY FRIENDS

I can hear grown-ups' feet
walking past me in my street.
Can hear them talk while passing by
beyond the realms of children's play.

Beyond the realms of make believe
I search the shadows grown-ups leave.
Shapes they once comprehended
now simply memories their mind has blended.

Ah, I hear them say, 'Only childish play!'
Yet to one who sees 'A world far, far away'

Destined are we to walk together, yet rarely ever
meet,
on a different journey on the same street.

BLUE EYES

Little girl
with eyes so bright
sleeping soundly
through dark of night,
laughing gaily
through light of day,
living wonder
carry me away
to a land unicorn still dwell;
where dreams can still
come true;
so innocent in your
world of play where
everything is new.

Reliving my youth again
through your eyes
of blue.

LONELY BOY LOST

Let me sleep,
please let me sleep,
for I have many friends to meet,
many friends who inhabit sleep.

I have dreamt them,
I have seen them
as they have dreamt and seen me.
Is it in my dream or in their dream
that we play so gleefully?

We form a ring, then dance and sing,
clap hands and count to three.

I hide in your dream,
you hide in my dream,
my friends play hide and seek with me.

Let me sleep,
please let me sleep
for I have many friends to meet;

many friends who inhabit sleep.

THE ROCKING HORSE

There is in each of us a memory
of childhood dreams and fantasy.
A voice may say, "Leave the past behind."
But I cherish life where life be found.

I looked into your room today,
you looked back at me as if to say,

"Do you remember we used
to journey together
over hill and down deep dale
in every type of weather?"
But now I rock myself to sleep
now you have grown.
No appointments left for us to keep,
now that childhoods gone.

I ask only,
"Do not let your love outgrow what once was
precious:
"Yes, you know!"
And do not grow tired of older friends
when new ones come along.
For friendship grows with time, you know,
and with time alone I have to spend.

"Please remember me, my friend."

A YOUNG BOY SITS

Upon a rock a young boy sits staring out to sea.
In front of him lies his future years; behind lays
history.

As if one thought were not enough
another thought appears
and he wonders what the future holds;
how long he has in years.

As he watches, the tide comes in.
Inexorably times sand disappears.
Behind, evening shadows increase;
with them comes a sombre peace

that as a blanket covers him.

A CHILD IN PAIN

How could one resist that cry?
The tormenting wail assaults the air.
She is so frail, so very frail
and in so much need of Daddy's care.

She needs a Daddy's long embrace,
simply knowing he is there.
She needs her Daddy night and day:
Only Mummy can compare.

She cries out in the night's long wait.
He holds her in his arms.
The healing she needs is in his grasp:
Her stormy trial only he has the power to calm
and he leads her from all harm.

SELF-RESPECT

She plays a game
but never wins.
Her confidence is low.

She needs a hope,
a little hope,
to help her
confidence to grow.

A little win,
a little step
forwards into self-respect.

THE BATTLESHIP

Floating upon a crystal screen
the battleship was floundering,
wallowing in a weedy pool:
Not really a battleship at all.

KALEIDOSCOPE

Prism of light,
colours so bright
coalesce within
consciousness,
impress on
my sight.
Shapes form
in my mind,
too many
to find.
Need to
follow the
patterns
as they
unwind
around
in a
spiral,
around
and
around,
spiralling
colours
bloom
into
flower.
Some

colours
tinker
with the
senses.
Other
effects
are more
psychedelic;
profound,
invading
consciousness,
relieving
stress,
helping
me to
cope,
giving
me hope.

All this
from
peering
through
a child's
kaleidoscope.

CATERPILLAR

Today she took a caterpillar for a walk.
Not a real caterpillar, silly!
Real caterpillars rarely talk.
No, not a real caterpillar
but a toy one with a plastic body
and coloured beads for legs;
a metal spring antenna
that seems to grow out of its head.

It follows her on a long piece of string,
after each step making a clicking noise,
sometimes a gentle clonk as it
defies the gentle pull of gravity,
slipping off the pavement
to fall at least four inches
into the waiting arms of a child
who believes it is real;
really, really believes that this life-form breathes.

I wish that I could so easily believe
that toy caterpillar's also grieve,
as well as walk and talk and feel.

LONELINESS

Loneliness lingers on in the heart of every boy.
As hours drift by in parents' sleep
he wrestles with his toy.
For no one wants to share his play
and he in anguish reflects in tears
the burden forced upon his back-
It is the loneliness of fear.

Drab old walls close in
and firelight has an eerie glow,
when you are alone, as a child,
at a time when loneliness can grow.

TEDDY

Teddy in her bed waiting for the day
that through her life will with her stay.

All through the dark of night she
holds him from all harm.
Nothing more secure to her
than Teddy in her arms.

Through the window morning comes;
she looks to greet the day.
With Teddy in her arms
she holds the world at bay.

THE CIRCUS CAME TO TOWN

The music filled my mind with memories of
another time and the smell of straw and thrills
galore.
Colours filled my sight and I was deep in awe
at the clown's first fight as they ran into the big top
and threw a bucket of slop
that turned into confetti in mid-flight.
The bloke in front got in a strop;
he gagged on paper, and blew his top.

The circus came to town every year.
You could tell it had arrived
with the change in the atmosphere.
I walked with daddy, hand in hand
and he lifted me up into the stand.
Everyone talked, all at one time,
but a hush descended as a bugle blew
and horses ran into the ring as if they flew.

My young eyes spied a young girl's form.
My eyes popped out; my heart became warm.
She wore something my sister would never have
worn;
so brief and simply too tight,
yet a young boys dreams were born that night.

I watched in fright and awe
as the men on the high trapeze

swung as Tarzan from the trees.
Without the need to cry out loud
they mesmerized the crowd.
Then came the acrobat tumbling along,
his muscled body contorted to a young girl's song.
Yet it was simply amazing to see a man
with only a cane step into the lion's den
become a hero from another age.
He was immortal and my life had become so strange.

A man then walked the tightrope of fear
and the crowd let out an almighty cheer.
I'd never experienced it's like before.
I was a child, and I wanted more.
Maybe one day I would be joining a circus,
become part of the show. I certainly hope so.

The end had come and I was tired,
we passed the caravans lined outside
and walked back home, yet in a way
I've never left the sensations of that circus day.

I will never forget as long as I live
the magical pleasure that it gives
someone with an impressionable mind,
who questions not what he finds.

The years have passed and so have circus ways,
with so many thrills how can it compete these days?
Yet in my mind the artists twirl and the lady whirls;

my senses opened and I reached out
and found a wonderland where there was no doubt,
only the thrill that rises from within,
when you realize that in this life something is missing, yet only by becoming a child can one attain
the big top of our imagining's again.

FUNFAIR

"Let us go to the fair, Daddy."
"Please, please let us go.
You promised me some time ago."

Hand in hand they walk
through a glittering archway
alongside candyfloss vendor and the hoopla stall.
Too many impressions on a young mind;
they all coalesce together in smells, colours and
laughter.

Hurdy-gurdy music sets the heart aflutter,
music of the carousel, music of the dodgem cars,
music of instruments, exotic dancers in the big
tent,
music played on a banjo and dance
music recorded long ago.

Balloons and kites made of foil,
cuddly toys as winner's prize.
A coconut from a shy-
All these are marvellous to a young child's eyes.

Down the helter-skelter;
round and round you go
until you slide to a halt with a bump,
coming to the end of the slides flow.

Up and up goes the scenic railway,

up and up to the clouds so high
then down and down almost to the ground
only to rise again up into the blue of the sky.

Screaming for all you are worth,
screaming as you have never screamed before,
screaming, because of fear of falling,
holding tight to Daddy's hand-
He will never let you fall!

"Daddy, the people look like ants from up here;
can you see them crawling?"
"Yes, my son, they do a bit."
"I can see the church spire of the town
from here and the clock says 6 o'clock and
we must be home for tea."

"We can come again tomorrow and bring Mummy."

FIRST DAY AT SCHOOL

It doesn't seem that long ago
the years just fly by
and my little girl
who I watched being born
brought a teardrop to my eye,
and still can make me cry.
For she is better than I ever dreamed
and older than she seemed,
dressed up to go to school,
bright as a button,
no longer small but bursting
with life and expectancy;
I suppose that is how she is meant to be,
if she is meant to be anything at all.

(Katy and Debbie first day at school)

FOUR WEEKS OLD

Four weeks old -

Only a spec in the vastness of infinity,
small as small can be
but every moment growing larger;
every moment developing
her unique print upon the human race.

Her own special personality
enriching this globe
and I am stunned that so much potential
is wrapped up in such a fragile a frame.

So much love that in the future
will burst forth from her like a mighty river,
flooding this world with her Katy song.

MY DAUGHTER ALWAYS

Remembering fondly her little smile,
her tiny fingers touching my lips,
her giggling laughter in my ears
and the way she holds her head aslant
so that she can better hear.
Her blond hair curled down her back,
her soft complexion shows no lack,
her ascendancy to my hearts throne complete.

Today, that child has gone away,
yet at times when she forgets
she casts all her cares at bay
and I see my little daughter yet.

Her blond hair still curls down her back,
her soft complexion shows no lack,
her laughter still causes the sun to shine,
her lips still red as ruby wine.

Yet she will always be my little Katy yet
and I must love her so, and not forget.

LONELY BOY

Loneliness lingers on in the heart of every boy.
As hours drift by in parents' sleep
he wrestles with his toy.

For no one wants to share his play
and he in anguish reflects in tears
the burden forced upon his back:

It is the loneliness of fear.

Drab old walls close in
and firelight has an eerie glow
when you're alone as a child,
at a time when loneliness can grow.

THE SANDPIT

All children need a helping hand.
All children need a pit of sand.

He sits alone, shovelling sand
into a sky-blue bucket from which
he creates the castle walls
around himself to keep his enemies
and tears and fears away.
It's his way of never getting hurt again
for he has suffered rejection and pain
and doesn't want to walk that path again.

He builds the castle around his heart.
He builds it thick and high from the start
yet prays for a friend to tear the walls apart
so, help him open wide the castle gates,
scale the treacherous castle wall so
bring healing to his heart that over time
has suffered, only to fall.

He needs a friend, who will catch him if he were to
fall.
A friend who will help him become confidence
again
and take away this interminable pain.
He is young and so very, very small;
only a little boy, after all, with a tremendous
dream.

A little boy who has lost his self-esteem;
a little boy desiring only friendship from another boy
to help him build the kind of toy that
needs not just one, but two of them.

All children need a helping hand.
All children need a pit of sand.
He builds and hopes for better things
until out of the corner of his eye
he sees another little boy.
A little boy with bucket and spade in hand
who asks, "Can I help you play with sand?"
He nonchalantly replies, "Please come and play, for
we have much to do today"

He will not turn this little boy away,
for all children need a friend to play with them
and build a castle of their dreams,
with open drawbridge that lets other little children in.
All children need a helping hand.
All children need a pit of sand.
All grow-ups have forgotten how to play.
They need pit of sandpit and a friend
who understands and will help them through their day.
A friend who will lead them by the hand
and will never, never walk away.
All grown-up children need a helping hand
to help them build dream castles in the sand.

THE SNOWMAN

It was
the first
snow she
had ever seen.

She was only five
and almost every year
that she had been alive
she stood at the window
expecting to see snowflakes
float down out of the sky.

Before today she had always
been disappointed.
Today was to be a different day.
She expected it to snow,
as if it were her present
for waiting so patiently.

She threw back the curtains
and I saw wonder in her face
as she saw her first flakes of snow.
She now knew what only
a little girl or boy can possibly know,
that there is nothing for a child
quite like the sight of snow.
Nothing is quite the same

as rolling a snowball down a lane.
Nothing seems so right
as an all-out snowball fight.
And to make snow grow into a man
with round brown stones for eyes and nose,
a twig for a mouth and gloves for hands.

She looks out of the window
most every day to see if her
snowman has melted away.
And one extra warm day
the snow magically turned into sleety rain
and the snowman along with the snow
is washed with all other snowmen
uncaringly down the nearest drain.

For to her, you see, her dreams
had melted and faded away.
But maybe next year
when more snow does appear,
her snowman may stay.

MEMORY IS A FUNNY THING

Walking along this canal tow-path
is like travelling back in time.
I remember two little girls
scampering along the toe-path ahead of us.
One with a blond pigtail;
the other with brown hair, tied back in a bow;
both giggling gaily, full of mischief and vitality.
The spring echoed with their laughter
as they ran helter-skelter ahead of us;
their destination an old brick bridge.

Each had a leaf which they dispatched into the
warm air to fall down into the scummy canal far
beneath them.
Passers-by showed wry amusement at this
treasured scene. Ducks and swans veered to the far
bank,
seeking the shelter of willow fronds.
A kingfisher spectacularly dived, hopeful of a
meal.
Dragonflies skimmed the water's surface;
Water boatmen rowed across on spindly limbs
as streaming Tench bubbles pricked the murky
waters.

'Hi Daddy, hi Mummy' our children cried out in
unison.
'Hi Katy, hi Debbie' Shirley and I chorused
together.

Now, with greying hair and little of that

I look down from the self-same old brick bridge,
see four women taking tea on an old narrow boat.
Their smiles are infectious for they are obvious
glad to be here.
On the bank a father, holding his young sons hand
walks proudly by.
A fleet of graceful swans spread ripples in their
wake.
The blue streak of a kingfisher implodes the water
and just as quickly, with fish in beak, returns to its
perch
high in the arms of the willow tree.
A Water Vole swims across the flow from its
sanctuary beneath a bank of roots and earth
and in my inner ear I seem to hear my darling
daughters cherished voices.

The gentle insistent voice of reason tells me it
cannot be so but my heart tells me a much more
tranquil story:

Memory is a funny thing.

MOVING PICTURES

Memories do not gather dust in my head.
They are like the reel of an old-time moving
picture,
forever showing at some antiquated flee pit,
where I called Home.

I see a boy of six catching a ball from his dad
outside a barber's shop in Lind Road,
opposite Jenny Lind pub.
His face is alive with the joy of youth
and the gratitude at being loved.

Another screening opens in the theatre of my
mind.
I am transported to a river bank
where rushes wave in the breeze
and cuckoos and blackbirds
make their distinctive calls.
Swans glide like a flotilla of great sailing ships.

My float submerges like a submarine
and I yank upon my rod.
A perch mysteriously appears by magic
in my landing net and my smiling dad
cheers gleefully, encouraging me for my good
fortune.

All memories linger from childhood,
fresh to the cortex of my brain,
the enduring pleasure of being young,
playing every day anew again and again.

THE FIRST TOOTH

Katy's first tooth fell out.
Look, Daddy, what I've got?
she said, sounding ever so proud.

I said, 'You are a brave girl'.
'Put it under your pillow
and in the morning, you will
be rewarded for your courage.'

'But will that morning ever come?'
   Katy said,
'I can't wait that long; what will I get,
O will it be much?
'O I'm so excited, ever so much!

The first tooth is such a cherished moment
to capture in time,
and to experience it again in
your very own child
is probably one of the greatest rewards
you can expect out of life.

GIRL IN THE CORNER

There is something unique about a smile.

She, standing in the corner of our room
captured as she is now for a little while,
dependant for only a short period of time,
yet as fragile as a flower in bloom.
Welcoming our attention yet delightfully coy;
posing for a picture still.
I love you as you are and always will.

The restless waves of time moving you forever forward;
each purposeful pose precious; filtered by memories.

Can I hold you in my hands, so stop times ravages?

No! We are times passengers moving together
between stations within another's carriages.

THE BLANKET

O what it is to depend
upon a blanket
as a friend.
A little friend
imaginary,
yet for her
just as real
as you or me.

O if only it were
so easy
for the likes
of you or me
to find a friend
so easily.

GET ME UP CLOCK

I want a get-me-up-clock;
a clock that gets me up.
It can tell the time, as I cannot
and ding the bell when time is up.
My ding-a-ling get-me-up-clock!

It has a face just like the moon
that the cow jumps over
and the little dog barks
and fiddles a tune and I
stop the clock and turns over.

A LITTLE BOY

My seadog day
and seadog night
make little waves
which must be right.

My head is churning
with the sight
of seadog day
and seadog night

While on the horizon
a ship appears
to drift casually
across all my years.

The blue of sky
and blue of sea
cast magic within
this heart in me.

Lost in wonder,
lost in joy
to know freedom
of a little boy.

WALLPAPER

Little boy with eyes so bright
dreams of goblins in the night.
Little children all must pray
and be tucked up in bed at close of day.
  There is another world, though paper thin.
  Remember that when wallpapering.
  That your paper on the wall
  may frighten someone very small.
Maybe only a fairy glade by day,
at night a goblin carries him away
into his lair, where're that be,
snaring little boys like me.
  Maybe it's safer just in blue.
  At night that becomes a nightmare too.
  A simple picnic with some bears
  can leave a little boy very scared.
At night dreams can come true.
Listen not to noises new.
Better to be slumbering very soon
than listening to a creaky room.
  I remember long ago Daddy held me longer so
  that I would not be afraid when shadows form.
  So, he held me till the morn.
For little gremlins grew in my mind
until I knew what I would find.
The only way to be alright
was leave a light on in the night.

A CHILDHOOD INCIDENT

Where have I left that innocent smile?
Down some back alley I used to kick a ball about
and play with my plastic rifle,
pretending I was a war hero
or Davy Crocket of the Wild Frontier,
or the Lone Ranger with Tonto in tow,
or Billy Wright of football fame.

The yard had all pervading smells
from the mess our dogs left
and smoke from chimney's nearby,
and washing being squeezed through the mangle,
and the smell of fresh baked bread from the corner
shop.

In the yard I dug for worms for the weekend
fishing trip
where I got covered in dirt from head to toe.
'Dirt never hurt anyone' that was our motto.
Then mum would call me in, handing me a
shilling,
asking me to buy a loaf of bread from the corner
shop.
If I was quick, I would get a penny for myself.
I ran like Roger Banister. I flew like Superman. I
zoomed like Rocket Man.

The yard was wet from overnight rain,
and as I tore along the lane just thinking
of the penny I had to spend,
I would not waste a moment getting there,
to rush into the corner shop,
frantically searching for the money in my sticky
pocket
to buy the loaf of fresh baked bread.

I raced the last stretch of the yard,
running into Mrs Jenner from next door
who tumbled head over heels in a heap,
with the French loaf stuck under her arm.
My mum came to Mrs Jenner's help.
My mum grabbed the broken bread.
My mum tried to clip me across the ear,
but I was gone like a hare on a greyhound track,
with lolly and heart in my mouth
I dashed down to Peter's house to hide,
no doubt I would have to bribe him with a
gobstopper
and promise of a lolly besides.

When I think of those days
I wear an innocent smile,
wander in my childhood for a while,
know all over again my parents love
and thank God in heaven above
for all the magic captured there,
shedding a heartfelt tear at treasured moments,
so very dear.

CHILDHOOD MEMORIES

Childhood for me has always held cherished memories but also mind-bending fears; fears which caused irreparable damage to my young impressionable mind. Fears which I repressed and dared not attempt to look at. They were locked away; compartmentalised in a room in my subconscious. That child never grew up and emerged at time of deep stress.

Through terrible traumatic experiences in the Second World War my father suffered PTSD and I never knew at any time of day what person I was going to face. Over the years I have suffered a number of nervous breakdowns and only recently through a course of medication can I say that this spiral of manic episodes has been halted. All I want now is peace of mind. It is my mind that has down the years played tricks with me; my child within needs peace now to enjoy the sunny meadows and refreshing sea spray. Hopefully publishing these poems and prose will draw a line under experiences of my past and begin a new phase of creative thought and healthy living.

SWING

Little lady, why do you swing
out into this world of suffering?
And how is it that you swing so high
up into the deep blue sky?

The world has changed so much
since you were young;
though the swings the same
it has not swung.

Maybe your daughter will swing again
out into a world that has not changed:
Up into a deep blue sky
where life expectancy is high.

And all who look at you
as you swing
feel young again
and life is like spring.

In some inexplicable way
your youth is recaptured in a swing.

TREASURE

She looked so sad, so very sad,
like a slightly disarrayed Cindy doll.
Her head was held in her hands,
slightly askew as if she was trying
to place it back on her body.
One solitary tear hung down
the precipice of her perfectly positioned
cheekbone.
If only I had been there to catch her
as she swung too far out into the unforgiving air
and fallen in slow motion like a feather
yet hitting the ground like a stone.

Her cries were resonant and heart-breaking.
My arms that held her trembled.
She was like a fragile precious treasure.
Her future spanning the years before her,
full of promise, so full of promise.
I realized more than ever I needed her
with all her pains, whims and ways
and on her part, she needed me,
especially at this moment in time
to take her in my arms and wipe
her tears and fears away.

THE SECRET

There is a secret joy shared only by a little boy
or little boys who meet in secret places
while all around them the old-world races.
For you see they dwell in a different domain,
their world called by a different name,
made up from a limitless imagination:
Shared together on every possible occasion,

To them, now, is the most important time.
You feel so safe when the weathers fine
and the wood and lane you've travelled before
casts little, long shadows in memories store.

THE BOY IS NOW A MAN

The boy is now the man.
The man will always be the boy.
He sees his Father now as no one else can,
the understanding sky blue eyes,
unblemished skin, still in its prime,
body sculptured as a god,
humour subtle and sublime.

On fishing boat of rigid oak and steel
We brave the ever, fickle tide,
Waves caressing our outer hull
like a bridegroom to a bride.

The salt sea spray chills our skin.
The azure sky fills us with dread from within.
Mountainous grow the turbulent waves
as boat is tossed like a cork in the brine.

We had fished our fill, now prayed for the storm to
cease,
little knowing if the sun would ever again shine.
The torrid air reeked of stale sick;
all hand on deck sagged from each hawking strain.

Yet we were held in Poseidon's godlike grip,
knowing a fear, we prayed to never know again.

Yet the Captain looked unperturbed,

even amused by our apparent plight
as he took the wheel and brought us safe to shore;
at long last we were free of the torments of night.

We stood together on solid ground.
Healthy catches of mackerel, sea bream and
cod for our pain.
Dad comforting his sickened son;
promised we would soon return again.

The boy now in his autumn years
testifies to this fond yet tarnished
memories with his tears.
A beloved Father, passed away these fifteen years.

He looks on with sadness at the rusty hulks
seeing worthy reflections in memories stream
of a Fathers love, given form in a young boy's
dream.

REMEMBERING

Remembering, this Yuletide Eve
the memories that Christmas leaves
deep in the heart and in the head
memories I thought forever dead.

Memories of a wonderland in 61;
a Christmas time of magical fun,
beginning at the unearthly time of 3
around our festive Christmas tree.

There was Sis and me with eyes aglow
spying our presents beneath baubles and tinselled
snow,
there our names were written bold and clear.
'Hush' I whispered. 'Maybe there's a reindeer near?'

For our minds were filled with youthful awe
and could not trust the sights we saw.

Inside, we felt the joy of living.
We both knew the love of people giving.
We knew our parents love and care.
They taught us well our gifts to share.

The day of joy dawned crisp and white.
Our hearts were glad, our life felt right.
We fed on turkey through the day,
laughed and giggled at our play.

No disappointment threatened our calm,

for we were immersed in joys sweet balm.
Even Grandmas tea hit the right spot with
turkey sandwiches, Christmas cake, soda pop.

By evening, though tired yet content
our energies almost completely spent.
So, Mummy coaxed us both to bed;
hugging us tightly and kissed our head.

Remembering brings a thankful tear
even down from that faraway year
when we were children in our wonder age,
reams of adventures to be written on life's page.

A CHILDHOOD INCIDENT

My name is Phil, I am 9 years old (62 years ago), another lovely summer's day and thrill of being young and alive; more importantly the joy of not being at school. Holidays are bliss! I meet Alan and Peter at the bus outside Sutton railway station. Here they come, first Peter, scrawny, with his lips curled upwards in a smile, his yo-yo making walking the dog on the pavement. Alan closely followed Peter. Alan was of medium height and of a sturdy build. You could never say Alan was loud, I always found him to be a sensitive and faithful friend. He was shorter than Peter who was tall and gangly, quite a bit taller than me. Shorty, that's what they used to call me, otherwise known as Phil. We are comrades in arms, living out everyday adventures.

We are going to Colley Hill, which overlooks Reigate. A lovely stretch of hills called the Weald can be seen in the distance. Hidden by the hills is Brighton town by the sea, twenty miles away. Colley hill as well as Epsom Downs was our favourite place to go. I suppose it was because we very seldom saw another person so we could easily let our imaginations run riot. The red bus, number 13, pulled into the bus stop and we boarded as if it was our own personal rocket ship. We jumped up the spiralling stairs three at a time and plonked ourselves down the green tartan chairs looking forward with great expectation to the journey ahead of us.

"Where do you want to go?" the conductor asked, "Oh, Colley Hill please" I said, handing over one shiny shilling. My friends did the same. The conductor gave a pained expression, for the money was sticky from boiled sweets left loose in our pockets. The time glided by. First stop Belmont appeared, the chalk hills clearly visible from the top of the bus. Banstead came over the rise with its coniferous woodland where I set my slow worm free when I was seven. It was only five minutes later that we arrived at Burheath. As a village Burheath consisted of a few shops and several large hotels; but what really interested us boys were the two outdoor swimming pools. One of these was in the grounds of the Sugar Bowl Hotel and was open to non-residents for sixpence a person. What was unique about the pool was that it was fed by underground springs and was simply breathtakingly freezing. As you dived in you had to catch your breath because of the intense cold. Goose pimple came up on your skin like small mountain ranges. It was a hell of a trip. The Wayfarer Hotels pool was just an ordinary pool, which you paid eight pence for a dip. Heathland came almost to the road and a small pond could be seen from the bus. I loved this pond. Dad used to take me fishing in it. I couldn't say I caught many fish, and even what fish I did catch were small, probably stunted by the ponds size. Adders slithered around in the heath land, so you had to be careful where you stepped.

Ding went the bus's bell and we were off to our next destination. Sometimes the journey is more interesting than arriving at your destination. We were at Lower Kingswood shortly afterwards. From there it was easy to walk to Colley hill. We stopped at the newspaper shop to buy some sweets. Sherbet dips all round washed down with Tizer. In the shop we met Sheila who was the proprietors' daughter and she had with her a Boxer dog named butch.

Every time we came to Colley hill we popped into this shop and met Sheila; she was our friend from outside town and Butch was always good fun to have around. No one was as thrilled to be go out into the wilds than Butch, and he made his feelings abundantly clear by jumping up and down, nearly knocking Peter down and barking like crazy. Her dad was always glad to see us leave; I suppose we scared away his customers, what customers he had at least, for Lower Kingswood wasn't a very large place. Outside the shop Peter was sucking a sherbet dip, sticking his grubby paws in the sherbet and obviously enjoying the sugary taste. Alan was kicking an empty can to spam along the unmade path. We were lucky that it hadn't rained around here for weeks, for when it had the paths and tracks were almost impassable. We would have had to wear our boots, plastic Macs and headgear. We would look then more like we were at sea than stuck in the countryside in Surrey.

It was a hot day; no wind blew across our faces as we came to the end of the unmade path and continued on a narrow track between two fields. Chain linked fences kept cows from wandering into the track. Alan the previous year had been feeding a horse cube sugar in Chipstead Valley, nr Banstead, Surrey and the temperamental beast had chomped down on his finger nearly cutting it in half. Hardly surprisingly he became very wary of anything with four legs.

"Will that fence hold those cows?" he asked.

"Look, isn't that a hole in the fence?" Alan continued to say, looking petrified by this time.

"Of Corse it's not; now your being silly!" Peter said

"Scaredy pants!" Sheila said. Though I don't think she was being cruel, she only wanted Alan to come with us. Nothing affects a boy more than the thought of looking scared or weak in front of his friends especially a girl.

"I'm only kidding", Alan said, and continued to walk ahead of us, just fast enough so he would not seem like he was running. As for myself I had always like the sound cows made. The smell that whiffed from the fields was a different matter entirely and I didn't want to prolong the journey by dawdling.

"Beat you to the style" I said, starting to run.

Peter always without fail won in every situation that required speed. Alan was best at stealth though; he would slip in behind the lead runner and be protected from the wind, making it easier for him. When we played war on the downs Alan would creep around, using bushes, trees and even long grass as cover and have his arms around your throat before you knew he was there. Though obviously having four legs was a distinct advantage to Butch who arrived first at the style and continued to leap over it. Trust a dog to out leg a human. I ran alongside Sheila. Even in those days I considered myself to be chivalrous brought up as I was on stories and films of King Arthur and the Knights of the Round Table, much that it got me any favours later in life. It wasn't long before we were in the bluebell woods. How mysterious they seemed. Elms grew close together; close enough for squirrels to hurl them from branch to branch. I never saw a squirrel fall all the time I was watching. It was a fact of life, squirrels never fell, "Wow, aren't they smooth" Alan said in his charming rustic way which set us off guffawing uncontrollably.

Sheila fell over a rotting fallen branch as she tried to jump over it and grazed her leg. I stopped and washed the wound with some of our bottle of Tizer and carefully bandaged it with my sweet stained handkerchief.

"Thanks Phil" Sheila said, and I blushed. I didn't like to seem a sissy, yet at the same time it was kind of nice to be needed by anyone, let alone a girl.

Fungus grew from the dead branch and toad stalls littered the ground. It was very magical really. Our staple reading diet was the Folks of the Faraway Tree and we such was our imaginations we quite expected to come across Silky, Moon face or the Saucepan Man. With Butch in tow, we were literally The Famous Five. This was to be truly a great adventure. Crickets chirruped in the undergrowth and our feet made cracking sounds as we trod through the long grass. The cracking sounds came from fallen twigs. We were pretty heavy footed, not considering g the fauna we were destroying; so prevalent was it at the time; so rich and varied. I wonder to myself now how many species must have been destroyed, never to return to the wild. We all believed in Fairies and Goblins, so kept our eyes open for any signs of these mysterious folk. We walked for perhaps fifteen minutes, though at the time it seemed to last for hours. Peter always led the way for he was the tallest. He gave a low whistle when he saw the water tower rising up through the space in the woods like a vast prehistoric beast.

"Not far to go now" Peter said, as he spit out his chewing gum and immediately put a fresh stick of gum in his mouth. We were coming to the woods edge and would soon be crossing an invisible barrier onto a rolling grassy open space that was Colley Hill.

I had first seen this sight when I was three years old from my dad's shoulders and it never failed to thrill me. We five were Pathfinders like Fennimore Coopers Hawkeye. Life could not be better. We flew free, sprinting for the edge of the hill. First Peter would push ahead. Then Alan would pull him back with his strong arms and hurl himself forwards. Then I scampered up on his blind side and surged ahead, helped of course by Butch who snapped at my friends heals. Butch found this to be great fun.

"That's not fair?" Alan said.

"All's fair in love and war" I said. I continued to explain myself, I always liked to be understood when I spoke. "I heard it somewhere, but I've forgotten where".

After we arrived at the hilltop we sat and crunched humbugs, which Sheila had taken from her dad's shop. I must admit to be fond of humbugs, and Peter and Alan echoed that fondness. Sheila's taste was more for Fry's Chocolate Cream, which she was sharing with Butch. We were sitting next to a folly, which also was a memorial to people who had died in past wars. There was a refreshing water tap which was heaven sent because of our great thirst. Butch lapped at the dirty bowl beneath the tap getting us wet such was his enthusiasm.

As we looked across the hill you couldn't feel any emotion but awe. You could see for absolutely miles and miles. South was the coast at Brighton, which was hidden by the magnificent range of hills, known as the Weald. Dorking and Box hill was to the West of us. We loved Box hill and went there often. At the foot of Box hill was the river Mole that had stepping-stones across it. We managed to get pretty wet every time we went there. To the East of us were Redhill and the County of Kent. Little houses could be seen in Reigate valley and even smaller people who looked like ants from this high up on the hill. Some wisps of smoke from chimneys could be seen spiralling up into the air. A steam train puffed by below us; its smoke making Indian signals, at least to us who spent every Saturday morning at the flicks (pictures house) watching westerns; that's what it looked like. It was travelling in the direction of Dorking and all stations west. This was before Beecham decimated our railway network. Although there was a discernible mist and smoke in the valley, up here on the hill, the air was so clean that you could almost taste it. We were all starving by this time such was the effort used up in getting here. We took out our sandwiches from our packs and a bottle of Tizer. I took and passed it to my friends, stating with Sheila. Lady's first: my parents brought me up to show respect to the fairer sex. This was the days before women's lib. I had a juicy red apple, although at second-sight not so yummy, for a maggot poked his head out near where I was chewing. A look of disgust came into my face and I threw the unfinished apple down the hill. Butch raced after it, thinking that it was a game, and when he caught up with it chomped it down, core, maggot and all. "Ugh, you disgusting beast" we all cried out. He looked up at us in confusion seeming to say, "You can't waste good food, can you?" Flies were hovering over Butch's head hoping to nab a bit of the feast.

I had read a book recently called The Cave Twins which was about life in the south of England at the end of the ice age at the time when Britain became an island. I was fascinated by how people survived in those long distant times. Food had to be hunted and one had to be cunning to survive. We were modern cavemen in these hot and dusky days before the advent of the Beatles. So disgusting was our eating habits that we burped unashamedly, all except Sheila of course who was more refined. She made scathing remarks about our animal behaviour. Butch had come back up the hill from his adventure and was chewing voraciously at a bone, which Sheila had brought with her, he followed this by slurping some Tizer from Alan's cup, which brought a shout of disgust from Alan.

I had mentioned before about the mist and smoke in the valley. We didn't think much about pollution in those days. The smell of burning from coal fires and nicotine smoke from pipes and cigarettes were part and parcel of life in those days. My Dad smoked a pipe, the smell of which I thought was quite pleasant and looking back nostalgically I can't help thinking not only of his sense of humour, the way being with me brought the best out in him and his distinctly smoky smell. We sat talking together for ages about what we would like to do and where we would like to go. It was nearly mid-day and the sun felt hotter on our fair skins. Peter and Alan wore caps. I had a crew-cut, which my dad, who was a barber, insisted I had because he said "It will strengthen your hair, Phil. That didn't work as now I'm as bald as a badger. The heat went through my head to my scalp, making my head a pinkie colour. Most distasteful I thought. Sheila's hair was blonde, worn long halfway down her back. Looking back now I would say that she was pretty, though in those days you dared not admit your feelings, especially concerning girls. Alan made a paper plane and threw it into the air; it soared out of his hand and very impressively flew down the hill. We made our own planes from the Dandy and competed to see whose plane could go the furthest, Butch ran down the hill again, chasing them like he would a ball or a bone, and seemed disgusted when he found them to be only made of paper and highly inedible. It was at this time, after we had eaten and rested that we decided that it would be fun if we had a competition on who could reach the bottom of the hill first. "The first one who reaches the stream gets a Kit-Kat" Peter said. "So, who is going to be the starter?" Sheila asked. "You can" Alan said. "Thanks a bunch! But what about the Kit-Kat?" Sheila said. "Oh, very well, whoever wins it has to give Sheila a bite of it" Are we all agreed?" I said firmly. My friends reluctantly agreed. Sheila held up her hanky, which was pink and smelt of violets. "On your marks, get set, go" she said, as her hanky dropped onto the grass. We hadn't taken the steepness of the hill into account or the man rabbit holes that littered its surface. As we ran our legs turned like pistons in a car, going ever faster and more out of control the farther we ran. Something bad was bound to happen, and we suspected that it was also going to be very painful. Peter, though the fastest of us all was the first one to fall by the wayside. His foot dropped into a rabbit hole and he fell arse over tit, rolling over and over.

We didn't have time to witness his demise for we were equally in dire straits. I felt myself falling and at the last moment managed to throw myself to one side, unfortunately into a gorse bush. The pain from the thorns digging deep into my flesh was excruciating and made me want to throw up. It seemed like Alan was going to be the winner of the bar of Kit-Kat but Butch had other ideas and was at that moment colliding into Alans's legs, so catapulting him, with wildly flailing arms, into the same gorse bush as me. Disgusting animal we all thought; though despite our pain we were in stitches we were laughing so much. I quickly stopped laughing when I realized my predicament with gorse thorns sticking out of my face. I felt I would have to be like Alexander Dumas 'The Man in the Iron Mask', and would never be able to show my face again, so marked was I. Sheila was laughing like a drain but decided to take advantage of our distress and scampered down the bottom of the hill, after which she stood with her arms in the air claiming, so the bar of Kit-Kat. "Cheat, it's not fair!" we all said in unison. Yet when all said and done, we were friends and it didn't really in the grand scheme of things matter who won as long as that person shared some of their winnings. We were all bound together by each other's triumphs as well as misfortunes. The more time we spent together the closer we became.

The midday sun blasted down on us unpityingly Sheila's laughter drowned out all other noises on the grassy hillside. We were young and free. A day seemed to last forever. We only had eyes for the moment, the future having little meaning to us at that time. Each hour was precious and each new experience had its own special magic. We were children in Never-Never Land; our lives we thought at the time would be intrinsically linked together forever. How wrong can one be.

After that Summer, Sheila immigrated with her

family to Australia, I never saw or heard from her again. Alan went to Sutton East County Junior School with us but attended a different school when we went into seniors. Peter and I walked to Sutton West County Senior School together every day. In the holidays we got together again to play cricket in Manor Park or go to The Gaumont picture house, but by the time we left school at sixteen I had lost contact with Alan. Gangly Peter for a few years attended the same cycle club in Mitcham called The Tooting BC. At the age of nineteen my family moved away from Sutton to a houseboat on the Basingstoke canal at West Byfleet and I never saw Peter again. What about Butch you may ask? That's another tale entirely.

ACKNOWLEDGEMENT

I would like to thank the people who have helped me in encouragement and criticism over the years.

Alan Barrie
Karen Mooney
Pamela L Serrilla
June McFarland
Zelly
Colin Rowe
Susan McMurchry
Shirley Carmen

Anyone I have forgotten I will add to my next book. Thankyou all.

ABOUT THE AUTHOR

Philip Carmen

My name is Philip Carmen and I  live in Hampshire, England. My wife is Shirley. We have been married for 42 years. Our children are Katy and Debbie. Our grandchildren are Isabella, Owen, Anabel and Lincoln. My interests are reading, writing, drawing, painting, music and films. We both love nature and walk often and visit gardens. In the twilight years of my life, I have no regrets.

BOOKS BY THIS AUTHOR

Mountains And Valleys Poetry-An Evolution Of Beliefs

A Christian book of poetry and belief (with a smattering of prose and lifestory)

Printed in Great Britain
by Amazon

85986557R00122